Thekla's Jo

From Hamburg to the Highlands and beyond

By

Patricia Young

For my family,
Past, present and future.

Contents

Contents 3
Chapter 1 Luneburg 4
Chapter 2 Dalwhinnie. 13
Chapter 3 Glenfarclas, Valley of Green Glass. 16
Chapter 4 Carron, Craigellachie and Aberlour. 22
Chapter 5 Muir of Miltonduff 1958-1959 30
Chapter 6 New Elgin. 1959-1964. 37
Chapter 7. Hamburg 1959 43
Chapter 8 12 Muirfield Road 53
Chapter 9 Halkirk Caithness 57
Chapter 10 Return to Elgin. 61
Chapter 11. The Folks frae Elgin 77
Chapter 12 Haste ye back. 88
Chapter 13 Moss Lane East Rusholme Manchester 93
Chapter 14 Central Grammar School for Girls. 97
Chapter 15 Eccentric Eric 109
Chapter 16 The swinging sixties 116
Chapter 17 Richard Barry. 124
Chapter 18 Mather College of Education 135
Chapter 19. Moorland Road, Didsbury 142
Chapter 20. Brandon Avenue, Heald Green. 145

Chapter 1 Luneburg

My tiger mother, Thekla Carla Dorothea Schultz, was born on 8th of August 1922. Perhaps with her Leo birth sign she would be better described as a lion mother as she was definitely fiercely overprotective of her offspring. She weighed two and a half pounds and was kept firstly in a shoe box and then in a drawer. She was the third of four children, Hildegard, Elfriede, Thekla then Kalli. They lived in Hanseatic city of Luneburg in the state of Lower Saxony.

Karl was an engineer in the Hamburg shipyard, and, after the Second World War he worked for the Mercedes Benz Company. Mum adored her father but always had a difficult relationship with her mother. They seemed to have a happy childhood. On photographs they all looked very well dressed and even then they had a car. It was one of those, with a running board down each side. Mum told us very little about her school days apart from the ink monitor at school dipping her plaits in the ink wells. Like the rest of the family she was the blond haired blue eyed Arian, even though there was Spanish and Mexican in her father's blood.

In 1933 Hitler came to power. He had already written two volumes of Mein Campf, meaning "my struggle" or "my battle." In chapter 14 he wrote "Germany will either be a world power, or will not be at all." He had already been exerting his influences on the German people and it must never be believed that they were accepting of his regime. Thekla was 11 when she became part of the Hitler Youth which was a paramilitary group of the Nazis. It started in 1922 but Thekla would not have joined till it became mandatory.

It was not a matter of choice but part of the dictator's efforts to demonstrate the cultural superiority of the German nation. She was one of the many blonde haired blue eyed children who sang for Hitler. He had a great love for singing especially the opera. When Mum was an old lady I asked her how she felt about this. Tears ran down her face and she said she felt ashamed. How can you be ashamed when you are a young child and these things are forced on you? In fact, it was supposed to be an honour. The Germans had a great musical heritage – Beethoven, Schumann, Mendelssohn, Brahms, Liszt and Wagner. I had always assumed opera was Italian but Mozart wrote The Magic Flute and Beethoven wrote Fidelio. They still cash in on this with chocolate wrapped in foil featuring Mozart. It's everywhere!

During the reign of Hitler, he decreed that women should not work so the many thousands of professional women were forced to give up their jobs and become housewives. Men took up the mantle of the work. Only much later in the war, when there was a shortage in the workforce, were some women encouraged to work in specific roles.

Hitler told the German people that the Jews were being repatriated to Israel and perhaps the people believed him until the evidence became overwhelming. Mum knew about the barrels of gold fillings and teeth and the skin lampshades. I don't think she knew that tattooed skin was the most favoured and chosen to order.

Thekla was 17 when war broke out and shortly after that, like many women, she went to work in the Land Army. She enjoyed her work there but she was innocent and did not know the facts of life. Thea never told any of her children, so when she was kissed by a boy she was worried she was pregnant. It was left to other girls to tell her the truth. I'm sure this is almost unbelievable nowadays but they did believe in storks delivering babies, and Luneburg is full of storks perched on chimneys.

She would have been well fed in the Land Army. Rationing came into place in 1936 so that resources could be used to fund the war effort, so a farm was probably one of the best places to be. Thekla gained weight living off the fat of the land but the same could not be said for less fortunate Germans. Mum told tales of people guarding the cabbages in their garden at night as well as during the day as food was a precious commodity. Other anecdotes told of people swapping gold, diamonds and emeralds for butter. I had visions of people in ermine stoles and coronets wandering round the street touting their baubles for cabbages and carrots.

Luxury goods were hard to come by during the war. There were no stockings so Kalli used gravy browning to tan his sisters' legs. The straight seams were made by each sister standing in turn on the table while Kalli eyebrow pencilled in the lines. Thekla loved her brother very much. She remembered when he came back from the war the family went to meet him at the station and they did not recognise him because he had grown a foot taller.

During the war she met Hartvig, a German soldier. They fell in love and he gave her a silver ring with a big blue stone and told her it was the colour of her eyes. That was the ring I wore at my wedding for something blue. It was a cheap paste and silver ring but sentiment has kept it in the family and now, my daughter Grace wears it.

Mum became pregnant and when her mother found out she locked her in a cupboard for three days, as a punishment for bringing disgrace on the family. Hartvig stood by her as did his mother Nana. Tragically Hartvig was killed on the last day of the war so when Rita was born she was given up for adoption. Rita, my half-sister, who I left it too late to trace. There have been many programmes on TV depicting mothers who had to give up their children at birth, so, I think today's generations may understand the cruelty of this a little better. Mum did meet Rita again but the meeting did not go well and mum was left with the feeling that she had not been good enough for her. We will never know whether this was right or wrong.

In Nazi Germany women were encouraged to have children outside of marriage. They even had Lebensborns which were buildings where selected unmarried women could go to get pregnant by a racially pure SS man. The buildings were openly publicised and they had a white flag with a red dot in the middle to identify them to the public.

One of the earliest laws Hitler passed was The Law for the Encouragement of Marriage. This was to encourage people to have as many children as possible. They were given an interest free loan when they married. If they had one child, then they did not have to pay back 25%. So, if you had the optimum four children then the loan did not have to be repaid.

After the war the German economy was in shambles. Twenty per cent of the housing had gone due to Hitler's scorched earth policy which is a military strategy involving destroying anything which could be useful to the enemy whilst advancing or withdrawing. Food per capita was only 51% of the level it had been in 1938. The food rationing set by the occupying powers varied between 1,040 and

1,550 calories per day and rationing continued until 1945 and as I mentioned barter was common. The farmers must have done well as they had the most precious commodity. After the war, Mum analysed food for the British soldiers. Odd then that Rita went on to become a pharmacist.

At the end of the war, not all servicemen were sent home at once. Germany was divided up among the allies. Forces were needed in occupied zones and there would have been too many unemployed men if they were all released at the same time. The British Zone of Occupation in 1945 constituted Schleswig-Holstein, Hamburg, Lower Saxony and North Rhine Westphalia. The British Army base was at Bad Oeynhausen under Field Marshall Montgomery. My cousin Rolf now lives in this area called Einhaus – meaning one house.

In 1946 there was an easing on the ban on marriage between British soldiers and German girls but they were not given permission to bring back and marry German women until 1947. Then they were encouraged to marry a soldier.

There were engagement parties in many parts of the British Zone. There was a great deal of red tape to get married then. After you had applied to get married there was a wait of at least six months. The main concern of the British Government was to avoid hardship on illegitimate children born to German women. A typical reaction was, "It has come at last. Now I can go to England". There was a shortage of young German men and they were hugely outnumbered by women until 1947. The German women were actively encouraged to marry men in the allied forces.

Mum had a good sense of humour, fun and mischief. She told us how she emptied a railway carriage by taking out her hard and extremely smelly cheese. It was actually a Swiss hard cheese called Geska, and boy is it stinky. She also told me that a woman had come onto her on a train. Mum was not impressed and must have had little knowledge of lesbians.

I loved the forties glamour photos of Mum posing against a wall with one leg bent up the wall, with or without hat. Many of the photos are signed with a soft pencil by the photographer Alice Brand.

Mum told us she used to be able to swim but some boys threw her into the sea once and she hadn't been able to swim since. She also talked about at least one other man in her life that she was fond of. His name was Bruno Schultz and he was a local police chief.

My father was in the Seaforth Highlanders. I suppose he looked quite handsome with his uniform, great coat and boat shaped glengarry hat. Mum told us that she had only known my father for a couple of months but we have found photographs with tender dedications on the back indicating she must have known him for at least two years. The allied forces were there to help the population recover after the war

Thekla, then aged 26, married Peter Young in Hamburg on May 15th 1948 in Blankenese, Hamburg. She didn't look happy even on the wedding photographs. Peter was a good looking man, about 5ft 7ins tall, with brown eyes and black hair slicked back with a quiff. This was a very popular way for men to style their hair. It was also known as a DA because the result looked like a duck's arse! He was well built with muscular arms and square shoulders. He had very bushy eyebrows which almost met in the middle. We found a photo with the dedication on the back saying "to my little Peter from your big Thekla." Mum was five foot three.

Mum had a beautiful lace dress with long train. Her mother and father were there, as were Elfreide and Kalli and our Gross mutter (grandmother). Elfreide's son Rolf was a page boy. I presume her parents approved of the marriage.

They got the train from Hamburg to Sylt which is a tiny island in Schleswig-Holstein in northern Germany which is joined to the mainland by a causeway. It was an RAF base during the war. It has its own microclimate and is in the gulf stream. Now the rich and famous holiday there but then, thousands of newlyweds went there as it only took 3 and a half hours from Hamburg. I can remember Mum loving cleaning a brass tray with bits and pieces on all saying Sylt. It was in our house for years. People have more interesting things to do with their time now than use filthy Brasso to make brass gleam.

Peter told Thekla there was a house in Scotland waiting for her. On the long sea crossing from Hamburg Hafen to Leith, Thekla had plenty of time to wonder what her future had in store. They could not speak much of each other's language, which added to the challenges she was about to face.

All she possessed were the contents of one suitcase and a book, The Rubyiat of Omar Kayan, which had been a wedding present. It was a beautiful book with loose illustrations by Dulac. The English translation of the text meaning "The moving finger writes and having writ moves on: nor all your piety nor wit, shall lure it back to canal half a line, nor all your tears wash out a word of it," but all of this would have had no meaning for Thekla, and very little for Peter who was not an educated man. I can't bear to part with it.

There were some people who were sympathetic and understood what the German people had suffered. Then there were others who wrote tongue in cheek songs. That's what Noel Coward did.

"Don't be beastly to the Germans"

We must be kind and with an open mind,

We must endeavour to find a way

To let the Germans, know when the war is over

They are not the ones who will have to pay

We must be sweet and tactful and discreet

And when they have suffered defeat

We mustn't let them feel upset

Or ever get the feeling that were cross with them or hate them

Our future must be to reinstate them.

Don't let us be beastly to the Germans

When our victory is ultimately won

It was just those nasty Nazis who persuaded them to fight

And their Beethoven and Bach are far worse than their bite

Let's be meek to them

And turn the other cheek to them

And try to bring out their latent sense of fun

Let's give them full air parity
And cheat the rats with charity
But don't let's be beastly to the Hun

We must be just and win their love and trust
And in addition we must
Be wise
And ask the conquered lands to join our hands to aid them.
That would be a wonderful surprise.
For many years they've been in floods of tears
Because for so many years
The poor little dears
Have been so wronged and only longed
To cheat the world, deplete the world
And beat the world to blazes
This is the moment when we ought to sing their praises

Don't let's be beastly to the Germans
When we've definitely got them on the run
Let us treat them very kindly as we would a valued friend
Let's be sweet to them and day by day repeat to them
That sterilisation simply isn't done
Let's help the dirty swine again
To occupy the Rhine again
But don't let's be beastly to the Hun.

Don't be beastly to the Germans
When the age of peace and plenty has begun

We must send them steel and coal and everything they need
For their peaceable intentions can always be guaranteed
Let's employ with them a sort of "strength of joy "with them
There better than us at honest manly fun
Let's let them feel there swell again and bomb us all to hell again
But don't let's be beastly to the Hun

Don't let's be beastly to the Germans
You can't deprive a gangster of his gun
Though they've been a little naughty to the Czechs and Poles and Dutch
But I don't suppose those countries really minded all that much
Let's be free with them and share the BBC with them
We mustn't prevent them basking in the sun
Let's soften their defeat again and build their bloody fleet again
But don't let's be beastly to the Hun

This was a satirical popular song in WW2 which was eventuality banned by the BBC as it did not translate well to radio. Churchill was said to have enjoyed the rendition of the song several times. It amuses me to know that Julian Clary now lives in Noel Coward's house and next door lives Paul O'Grady in his mansion with his menagerie.

After the war in 1945 Germany was split into two blocs – East and West. The east was known as the Deutsch Democratic Republic (DDR) whilst the west was the Federal Republic of Germany. The Federal Republic was divided into three zones of occupation by the Americans, the British and the French. This was known as the Potsdam agreement. The East was a communist state run by Joseph Stalin. Hildegard and her family were trapped in the East. There was a steady flow of refugees back to the West and in order to put a stop to this the Berlin Wall was built in 1961. Germany was not reunited until 1990.

Mum eventually managed to travel to the East to see her sister, having applied for all the relevant papers and passing through Checkpoint Charlie in Berlin but she was always afraid she would not be allowed back.

But here we are back in 1948 Mum arrived in the isolated outpost of Dalwhinnie.

Chapter 2 Dalwhinnie.

Dalwhinnie is one of the coldest villages in the UK with an average annual temperature of 6.60C, and snowfall is very heavy. It is an area for walking, mountaineering and of course skiing, with Aviemore being close by. Dalwhinnie is the highest elevation working distillery in Scotland and it is a remote location near Loch Ericht. It is in the Cairngorms National Park, which is teeming with wildlife. Dalwhinnie Railway station was completed in 1863 and is on the Highland Main line and the Great North Road. Its Gaelic means meeting place.

Mum arrived at the station which, to this day, looks more like a Halt than a station. I don't suppose any amount of limited knowledge she had of Scotland would have
prepared her for this special, beautiful, magnificent, bleak, moody and lonely place.
The distillery is in a flat basin, surrounded by mountains, which look like sleeping
elephants. White in the winter, purple with heather in the summer, and, in the spring, ochre with gorse. Here she was, and she must have wondered what she had done. She was a captive wife. Under Scottish law a wife belonged to her husband and had very few rights. He had lied
to her when he told her there was a house waiting for her. Instead she had one bedroom in her
in-laws' house. Peter senior and Mary, had five children in that house: Ian, Jim, Peter, Malcolm and Molly. The sons were all returning from war and the house was about to become overpopulated.
The in-laws found the situation equally difficult. They would not have been expecting
Peter to come home with a Gerry, a Nazi, or many of the other racist names which
followed us for many years to come. Mum did her best to fit in as she put five words under her pillow every night in an attempt to learn the language. Jim came home with Micky, or Michaela, as his new wife and Mum did not like her and I am sure the feeling was

mutual. Mum did not like the Greeks. In an ironic twist, Mum never knew that her own name, Thekla, was Greek. Her name over the years caused her so many problems. Most people could not pronounce it. She was called Theckla most of the time but at one time even as tequila. In hospital as a patient, there was always the phonetic spelling "taycla" above her bed. I never got to grips with how someone who was the victim of racism could go on to be racist herself Sorry Mum, but I did tell you several times.

In a modern day parallel, here we are repeating history. Most of the German people were not Nazis. Most of the Moslem people are not Daesh. Fear and bigotry blur lines and make us deeply suspicious. Exactly playing into the hands of the enemy.

Many of the distilleries had their own schools. All the Young children went to Dalwhinnie School. I found a photo of my father and his brothers, Ian and Jim, taken around 1920. It's unmistakably him. I have no photos of him as a child. He did fib to me, though. He told me they were all too poor to have shoes. Well, he has boots on in the 1920s so I suppose the rest was a fabrication - that the children only ever got the tops off the eggs, even though they kept chickens. Also that they got rats in their stocking at Christmas.

Dalwhinnie 15-year-old whisky sells itself as a whisky with a taste of pine needles and
heather, balanced with honey, malt and peat which are all local ingredients. The children grew up here and worked here. In the Visitors Centre there is a list of employees and their roles.
There is my grandfather, Peter Young, on the open page, as Head Maltman. I imagine all
the sons became maltmen and after the war this would have given them a modest skill.
I spoke to the archivist at Dalwhinnie, who was very helpful. Up until 2013, there was a
lady who remembered the whole family. Unfortunately, she was too frail to answer any questions.
It must have been difficult in the house so, given that he had the skills of a maltman, he got a
job. The distilleries would have been working at low capacity during

the war as the men
had gone to fight, and whisky was rationed so now was time to pick up the speed of making whisky again as it takes many years to let a single malt mature.

Chapter 3 Glenfarclas, Valley of Green Glass.

Glenfarclas is a Speyside distillery in Ballindalloch. It is in the Ben Rinnes mountain
range and sits in the moors of Banffshire. Glenfarclas is high above sea levels in the mountainous Cairngorm area. The distillery is one of the few to used aged sherry barrels.

Glenfarclas Distillery was their first home and the first of many tied cottages. It must have been another shock for Mum to find again she was in the middle of nowhere, with very
few people around and only a basic command of English. There was no running water,
and the well was in the back garden. Everyday tasks were extremely laborious. Water had
to be heated, a kettle at a time, on the range cooker, to fill the tin bath. The use of the bath
had a pecking order, with the head of the household being first, even though they would
have been the dirtiest. The range was the only heat source in the house. The house was lit
by oil lamps, and candles in the bedrooms. There was a need, rather than a desire, to be completely self-sufficient.
The range needed wood, so, Peter chopped down the trees and then they had to be sawed
into pieces on a sawhorse, which was a trestle arrangement to support the wood. The two-
man saw was constantly in action. Mum at one end and Peter at the other. It was hard work and had to be done in good weather, stored and dried for the winter. The logs then had to be chopped into kindling and firewood. In 1948 a quarter of British homes had no electricity and it must have been a higher proportion in outlying Scotland.

The baker's van came a couple of times a week to deliver bread and

Scottish morning rolls, called butteries. The butcher came less often. Wages were extremely low so meat was a rarity However, Mum liked her sausages. She didn't know what the word was so my father told her to ask for slingers or Paul Robeson's, who was an American black singer. There was a hidden meaning there which the butcher found highly amusing. As he got to know her he explained the trick which had been placed on her and explained the proper names. He probably felt sorry for her as she was certainly "an innocent abroad". Meat was rationed until 1954 when meat ration was about 100g per week and now we have that much each day.

I was born in Dufftown Cottage Hospital on March 28th 1950. All my clothes were knitted or acquired from someone else as cast-offs. When you live in a small community you rely on each other for help. At around 15 months old, I was vaccinated for diphtheria, which is an airborne infection causing particular problems in the throat, and can lead to the airways becoming blocked and can cause death. Mum said I nearly died and I certainly have a very nasty scar on my arm. The entire population was vaccinated. There are still a few cases of diphtheria today, but these have usually been imported.

One thing my father was good at was providing food. He was an excellent fisherman and a crack shot. He could snare rabbits of which, at least initially, there were plenty. The snares were made of a short stake of wood and a noose of wire, which tightened when the rabbit put his head in. Wherever we lived, there were shotguns and orange cartridges in the house. There were fishing rods and all the trappings needed to live the country life.
Waders for fishing, plus fours for shooting, game bags to carry the birds, huge nets to gather the fish, and of course the flies to catch the fish.

Mum had to learn how to skin and cure rabbit and moleskins. My father had to smoke out
the moles as a mole can dig up to 15 feet in an hour; they leave the roots of plants exposed
under the ground and therefore they die. They are neither the farmer's nor the gardener's friend.
I had a rabbit skin coat and a toy rabbit called Judy made from the rabbit skin with buttons for eyes. Nothing was wasted and the bobtail was a lucky charm. (Not lucky for the rabbit.) I had a moleskin muff and hat. Muffs have very little use in today's world. A muff is an open-ended cylinder of fur, which was tied with cord around your neck. You put your hands inside the muff to the keep them warm. They could be used for extra warmth with gloves. I wouldn't be at all surprised if muffs reappeared on the catwalk as the latest fashion must-have! The fur was black, soft and dense. In modern parlance a muff has a different meaning!

Moles are a real pest. They are attracted by worms. They can either be caught in traps or
smoked out with sulphur-based mole smoke. Not something on sale in Sainsbury's!
Rabbit meat was good and plentiful- until mixamatosis appeared. There were so many rabbits causing so much damage to crops that the government introduced the disease to control the rabbits and stop the destruction of crops. I remember the horrid death for the rabbits and there was no rabbit stew for many years after that. It was also at this time that the song *"Run rabbit, run rabbit, run, run, run, don't let the farmer get you with his gun"* became popular again. It was originally released to poke fun at Hitler, but was still popular at the time of mixamatosis.

Every commodity was valued, precious and recycled. Brown paper was ironed and
folded. String was rolled up and reused. Garments were knitted, unpicked and reknitted.
Clothes were resized and made into something new. Washing was difficult with no machines. All the fabrics were natural and harder to care for. Each house had a designated washday, usually a Monday. The washing was scrubbed on a glass scrubbing board, wrung by the

wringer and dried by the fire. It took all week to dry especially in wet weather.

The scrubbing board also doubled as a recognised instrument when used with thimbles played on the coarse glass. Mum brought with her from Germany her Honer Melodica mouth organ, which she played well. The other instrument was the comb. A sheet of thin paper, usually cigarette paper, was folded round the teeth of the comb. The paper had to be separated from the foil part. You blew on the paper, causing it to vibrate and make a sound and often it would tickle your lip. The silver part of the paper was then folded round your finger, removed, twisted to make a base and then hey presto – a miniature goblet. 1950s entertainment. I went into a pub as an adult as saw thousands of these goblets on the ceiling which must have had chewing gum on the end. I am imagining all these men having a competition to see who could fling and stick their goblets up. The walls were yellow and it must have been decades since they were decorated but that's exactly what it was like. Syrupy nicotine dribbling down the walls and not much better in people's houses. Yuk.

Mum became pregnant again and I had a brother called Norman. He was what they called a
blue baby and he lived for six weeks. It is only in researching this I found out one of the
causes of blue baby syndrome: nitrate contamination in the ground, resulting in decreased oxygen-carrying capacity in the haemoglobin in babies, leading to death. The nitrates could have come from fertilizers on agricultural land. There was agricultural land all around and fertilizers were untested and, crucially, our water source came from the land. I always thought, with a blue baby, it was some kind of blood disorder, and if you changed the blood all would be fine. Had we been near a hospital this would have happened.

My sister was born in Aberdeen hospital on 26th August 1953. I can only presume after the problem with Norman, she was advised to go to a large hospital. Fiona was robust, hale and healthy. I was not impressed! "Take her back, Mummy," I said. Mum was breast feeding Fiona. "Is she eating all that meat with no tatties?" I asked.

With no rabbits to snare, our food was supplemented with salmon from the River Spey,
and in season, pheasant, grouse and partridge and this was normal food for us. My father
would shoot the bird. Mum would gut it and pluck it and singe the last bits of feather.
Some of the birds had to be hung to improve the flavour. There were often braces of pheasant and partridges hanging to in the larder.

Winters in the highlands were tough, that's why there is good skiing at Aviemore. We
were tucked up in bed with blankets and anything else which was warm. I always had the
heavy, khaki army greatcoat and hot water bottles soon went cold. The windows iced up inside and it was fun scratching patterns in the ice. It's very easy to believe in tales of
Jack Frost painting the windows with frosty patterns. Often, during the winter, the snow
drifts would come right up to the bedroom window. We were really snowed in and so we
always had a shovel inside the house. My father dug a tunnel out of the house so that he
could walk in the deep snow to the distillery, which was just across the path.

One winter I had a really bad gumboil, like Algernon in my favourite Rupert the Bear
book. Mum put a tartan scarf right around my head and under my chin. You never hear of
people having gumboils nowadays, which makes me think it must have been some
dietary deficiency or lack of vitamin D.
As we were snowed in, and completely cut off from the rest of the world, the crew from RAF Lossiemouth dropped off food parcels for us. There were several small communities cut off like this. One of the crew dangled from
the helicopter winch, dressed as Father Christmas. Mum woke us to look out of our

bedroom window and see him and I remember it vividly.

The next day, Santa had left me a doll, one of the 1950s pedigree dolls with hand knitted
clothes and one shoe. Mum told me that Santa must have dropped it so Mum carried me
outside to look for the shoe, and there it was. Magic!
Every distillery had a customs and excise officer who tested and guaranteed the quality of the whisky and collected the taxes. Glenfarclas is very close to the Ballindalloch estate. This country estate has its own castle and distillery.

Chapter 4 Carron, Craigellachie and Aberlour.

We moved to Carron which is a tiny village on the banks of the River Spey. My father got a job on the beautiful Ballindalloch Estate as a gamekeeper and ghillie in the season. His job was to raise pheasant, partridge and grouse from young chicks and provide a good habitat for the birds. He also helped out during the red grouse shooting season, which starts on the glorious 12th of August.
His job as a ghillie was to show visiting fisherman where to fish on the River Spey and to give advice about tackle and tuition, especially in how to cast a line. The fishing on this famous river drew famous people. We had on our mantelpiece a picture of John Snagge. My father spent a long time with him and he was a famous radio broadcaster before and during the Second World War. He had a distinctive resonant voice and also did the broadcast for the Queen's Coronation. Mum was smitten as he was good looking and famous.

Our tiny cottage was on the banks of the Spey. There is a one of a kind road and rail bridge across the Spey. Mum told me years later this was where she jumped off the bridge in an effort to commit suicide. A passer-by fished her out and it's hard to imagine the depths of despair she must have been in to do this. Her life was her children, so the balance of her mind must have really been disturbed.

Carron, Aberlour and Craigellachie lie along the River Spey in a line from east to west. When I was old enough to go to school, it was a little too far to travel from Carron to Aberlour so we moved to Craigellachie. There is a cooperage here making barrels for whisky. A backhander to the lorry driver was all it needed for the little furniture we had to be moved.

Craigellachie is at the confluence of the River Spey and the River Fiddich which gives the name to the Glenfiddich whisky. It is walking distance from Craigellachie to Aberlour, and from Aberlour to the Distillery.

Although Craigellachie is a small village it has a bridge designed by Thomas Telford. At either end it even has mock-medieval towers with arrow slits and crenelated battlements.

The River Spey runs for over a hundred miles from its source to the sea and it's the fastest flowing river in Europe, falling over 1100 feet over its course. The Spey fishing season opens on February 11th and closes on 30th September. There is licensed fishing at Ballindalloch, Aberlour and Craiglellachie on the lower Spey. The salmon is known as the king of fish and Scotland, the home of fly fishing.

I watched a humorous film based on a book by Paul Torday. It was called *Salmon Fishing in the Yemen*. It tries to make you believe that if you have endless resources and a vision you can make the title possible. Of course you can't have salmon fishing in the Yemen and it was a disaster as Speyside salmon fishing cannot be replicated.

We always had guns in the house: a 12 bore shotgun and a .22 rifle. The shotgun was designed to be fired from the shoulder and it fired tiny lead pellets which embedded themselves in the game. Mum tried to get them out when she plucked the birds but this was not always possible and you had to be careful when eating to spit out the lead shot.

My father tried to teach my mother to shoot but the kick-back from the gun propelled her backwards and badly bruised her shoulder every time. The long .22 rifle was used for shooting small game. Shockingly, my father shot my mother's cat, McFlannel. He was jealous that she loved the cat and got rid of him dramatically in front of her. In some masochistic way he was wielding his power. I never felt threatened that he would do that to us and thankfully I didn't witness the incident.

I have fond and vivid memories of my time here as it was a safe and naturalistic childhood, the like of which it's very difficult to find now. I enjoyed it when my father took me fishing with him. It's a serious business and you have to be quiet. I occupied myself looking for wild flowers, or making grass trumpets. With a blade of grass held between both thumbs, you blow till it vibrates. It's one of the things the National Trust recommends should be part of childhood. I would run up and down along the banks looking for kingfishers. There were plenty of them and they always perched on overhanging branches to give them a good view of the fish in the river. They dived at speed and rarely missed spearing the tiddler with their long sharp beaks. Their colours are truly spectacular and to this day, one of my favourite colours is kingfisher blue. Since leaving Scotland I have only seen one kingfisher flying over the moat at Leeds castle in Kent. More than 40 years between sightings.

My father always wore his cloth cap and country jacket to fish and shoot. It was a Harris Tweed jacket with leather elbows that could be replaced. You can still buy these. One jacket would last the whole of your life. He had his green chest waders and big net to put the fish in. He had his reel and line and of course the flies. I remember the whizzing noise it made when he cast the line and it has a special name which is famous among anglers, the Double Spey cast. It was special because the anglers could not get the hook accidentally caught in bushes and trees. He did catch himself on a hook whilst fixing a fly. "Bugger," he said. I went home saying it and he told me it was the name of a fishing fly, and for many years I believed him. Swearing was a big no no so he was in trouble with mum.

He had all his salmon and trout flies in a tin. They did look pretty with all the feathers, and certainly did look like winged insects. The flies had the most wonderful names, Jock Scott, The Green Highlander, Hairy Mary, Silver Doctor, Dusty Miller, Stoats Tail, Gerry and Munro's Killer.

He caught salmon and brown trout, also known as sea trout. He would frantically wind in the line with some strategic stopping, and then go into the river with his waders and large net to put the fish in. The fish were beautiful iridescent colours. I remember watching the salmon going upstream to spawn. Salmon change from silver to pink when they are spawning. It is a great privilege to have seen such unique wildlife and countryside. Sometimes Mum and Fiona came and we had a picnic of "pieces," (sandwiches), and flasks of tea. It was idyllic. My parents kept their matrimonial difficulties away from us, at least for the time being.

Mum bought him a mug with the Anglers Prayer on the side.

"Lord grant that I may catch a fish,

so big that even I,

when speaking of it afterwards,

will have no need to lie."

Anon.

I'm sure he never needed to lie! The house was full of cups and trophies he won for fishing and shooting.

He was a heavy smoker, which was very common at this time. The movies glamorised smoking and then little was known of the dangers. He always had nicotine stained fingers. He smoked Senior Service some of the time, but rolled his own at others. I was fascinated by the rolling machine and the packets of Rizla papers. He used Old Holborn tobacco in a tin and it had a pungent smell that lingered in the empty tin for years. Smoking whiled away the hours waiting for the fish to bite.

Aberlour is the name of a town in Moray which flanks the Spey. Its full name is Charlestown of Aberlour and it often gets its Sunday best name. It was once the site of a famous orphanage which took orphans from all over the U.K. The Orphanage was split into two units, one for the girls and one for the boys. Between the two buildings was the school where the children were taught. If you had to live in an orphanage, then this was a good place to be with such beautiful surroundings. The Orphanage had several Royal visits. Edward V11 visited in 1907 and George V and Queen Mary in 1922. Balmoral wasn't far away.

It is also the place where the famous Walkers Shortbread is made and if my husband had known this, I think he might have moved north, rather than me moving south of the border.

Aberlour Primary School 1955-58.

While Fiona was at home with Mum, "eating all that meat with no tatties", I was riding on the crossbar of my father's bike to my first day at school. I loved it, and it's a good job I did seeing as I was going to spend the rest of my life on the other side of the desk.

I remember learning the alphabet, the letter names rather than the phonetic sounds. I wrote on some kind of little blackboard with chalk or slate. Paper was very expensive so it would have been considered a waste of money to give young children exercise books. All children were given a small third of a pint bottle of milk. The blue tits would peck the cream when it was frozen making the foil lift the top off. I hated the milk except when it was cold. It was full cream milk, thick and horrible, especially when it was warm. It put me off milk for life.

I learned to draw flowers and a bowl with perspective. I have never had another art lesson like this. There were two terracotta bowls, one filled with tulips and one with daffodils. We learned to draw the trumpet of the daffodils with pastels. The square pastels were a new and messy experience and the colours were so vivid. I was enthralled. I have often tried unsuccessfully to recreate the picture which remains in my head.

I had to walk home from school through the woods with my satchel on my back. The wood was marvellous. There were carpets of wild snowdrops, crocuses in purple, yellow and white, wild daffodils and primroses, hundreds of them, all naturalised on the forest floor. Later on came the carpet of bluebells. I was like Red Riding Hood and often strayed from the path. The snowdrops would have been a galanthophile's delight but it is illegal to dig up wild flowers. Snowdrop collectors pay hundreds of pounds for just one bulb with a slight variation and there are hundreds of them. They like to buy them "in the green" which gives the best chance of success. There were enough crocuses to harvest the stamens and dry them for saffron as we used to do in Saffron Walden. Yes, that's true, we used to have saffron farms in the UK.

In the summer there were shows. The men exhibited gigantic vegetables and flowers. There was always a children's competition usually for a miniature garden, made of a tin lid with a mirror for a pond, carefully selected moss and pebbles, and any small flowers I could find. I was always keen to enter and look at the exhibits and prize certificates and rosettes.

I went to Sunday School where Dr. Sellars presented me with a book called *The Toadstool Mountain.* Books were expensive and you didn't get many. They were a real treat, to be savoured and cherished. I had been practising my curtsey and executed it well. Dr. Sellars was lovely. She was the family doctor and very familiar to us and she always wore pearls. I coveted them and so began a lifetime of collecting pearls. Cream, Tahitian pink, black, grey, freshwater, cultured, baroque and even some blue ones from Borneo. If only I had known about the mussel pearls in the Spey, I would have had my own waders and gone collecting. The tiny mussels spend their first winter inside the salmon gills and they hitch a ride upstream. It does no harm to the fish. I would have been investigating every salmon my father caught and had a grow my own experiment at home.

At school I played with the children of the Customs and Excise officer. I have a photo of the three of us on a bench, all with hand knitted Fair Isle jumpers featuring a spaghetti of tangled wool at the back but a beautiful pattern at the front. This is a traditional knitting technique to create patterns with multiple colours. The Fair Isles are part of the Shetland group of islands. This is difficult knitting and would have required a high level of skill and experience to execute.

I played with these girls but not really with traditional toys. There were plenty of National milk tins, dolls tea sets and water. There were nearly empty bottles of horrid Camp coffee which was 4% coffee and mostly chicory. There were usually a few dregs to be added to water. Then there were a few spilt peas and lentils to cook in the saucepans. We played in the shed with orange boxes and tea crates as our furniture. Long before tea bags, tea was imported loose in crates. The grocers would decant into smaller packages and sell the crates. Tea crates were coveted for flitting. (moving.) We had an old babies bottle. The kind that was banana shaped with a teat on either end. Sometimes there were dregs of powdered milk left so we mixed this with water and put it in the banana! We had an empty perfume bottle which looked so grown up and glamorous. It was an inky blue bottle of Soir de Paris with an amber, spicy scent which still lingered in the empty bottle. It is still made today by Bourgeois in different packaging and it was the most famous perfume of WW2. It had a silver triangular label and a little silver dabber in the top. Children had very few toys so you use your imagination and whatever you could find. A real treat would be something like a packet of plasticise which had perfect strips of virgin colours till you used it.

Children are egocentric and I remember little of Fiona at this time other than being somewhere beside me. Little sisters are often an embarrassment and she was a tomboy and not interested in the same things as I was. Three and a half years make a difference to who you want to play with. She has not forgiven me yet for telling her she had milk in the back of her legs!

For a short time, in 1956, we had a car. My father couldn't drive and had not passed any test. Road testing was suspended this year because of the Suez Crisis and the examiners were busy administering petrol rations so he would have been legal to drive the 20-year-old Austin 7 box saloon. The car had been manufactured as one of the first cars for the working man. It was tiny with two front doors and a starting handle. The handle looked like hard work and seemed to take many attempts. The bonnet opened by folding in half and there were no indicators, so you had to use hand signals. It was exciting but at the same time frightening. We didn't have the car for long before I remember lying in the car in a deep ditch. Luckily we were not hurt and the car stayed there and we never had another one after that.

The next ride in a car was with Uncle Gus, who was married to my Auntie Molly. I loved them and their daughter Shona McGregor. We were driving round the notorious Devil's Elbow at night, with only the stars and the cat's eyes to illuminate the way. I was incredibly car sick, something which would follow me well into my adult life. This was the main road to Braemar, a journey Prince Philip has driven many times in his Daimler. Now this part of the road is not used. It was the highest road in the UK and a real white knuckle ride. I bet the Royal Family remember it. Mum must have felt "immersed in Scottishness", as Queen Victoria said. Only Mum hated it!

As a child you never question why you are moving again. It was such a shame, as this was the place where my father was in his element.

When I think about my father it is not with love the way it should be. It is more with fear. I don't remember any cuddles or closeness. There were memorable moments though. I always prayed before I went to bed and he taught me this prayer:
"As I lie down this night to sleep,
I pray the Lord my soul to keep,
If I die before I wake,
I pray the Lord my soul to take."
Although I said it every night it scared me. It is one of very few memorable moments. We never had a darling Daddy and for Fiona there was worse to come.
One day the minister from the Craigellachie Church visited Mum. Perhaps it was after her attempted suicide as he became a regular visitor and his wife sent Mum plants. We had a few hens here and they came in and out of the kitchen as they pleased even when the vicar was there.
Mum was not religious but she did teeter round the edges. She believed in life after death and any kind of spiritualism. She believed in horoscopes, palm readings, tea leaves and tarot cards, talismans and gypsy curses. She always carried a lucky black cat in her purse. Her lucky numbers were three, four, seven and eight. Any kind of superstitious clap trap that offered a glimmer of hope, escape and good fortune, to get her out of her desperately lonely and unhappy life.

Chapter 5 Muir of Miltonduff 1958-1959

Miltonduff is a hamlet a few miles out of Elgin in Morayshire. This is where my father went to work for the distillers George Ballantyne & Sons as a maltman again. He was involved in the malting of the barley which was soaked in water for two to three days then spread out to germinate. The process took about 10 to 14 days and the barley was regularly turned The germination process converts the starch in the barley into sugar (maltose) hence the name malting. The barley dried slowly over a peat fire, and was regularly turned to ensure even drying. It gave rise to many pubs called The Malt Shovel and the Maltings.

Some of the whisky here is called Miltonduff and some Mosstowie. One of the rare Mosstowie whiskies costs £550 per bottle. If only my father had saved it instead of drinking it, we would have been living in clover. The distillery gets its water from the Black Burn which flows into the River Lossie and then on out to sea. It is at this point where it joins the sea that generations of the Young family worked the land as crofters, ploughmen and grooms. Most of the women worked in domestic service.

Another tender moment happened here. My father took me to work with him. It was always nice and warm there but there was a howling wind outside penetrating and whistling through the building. He suddenly burst into recitation:

The north wind doth blow and we will have snow,
And what will the robin do then poor thing,
He'll hide in the barn and keep himself warm,
and wait till the coming of spring, poor thing.

I shiver for the robin now but I have never forgotten the poem. In my head there is a picture of the robin with his head under his wing. (Anon)

The distillery lies in the Glen of Pluscarden where there is a Benedictine Priory and the Catholic Abbey is the only medieval British monastery still being used for its original purpose. The monastery was close to where we lived. Fiona and I walked and hid around the outskirts but we were worried about being captured. We listened to the strange Gregorian chanting and were very careful not to be seen.

Our tiny tied cottage was on a little road with about 10 houses. The largest house was the first and of course it belonged to the Customs and excise officer but we were tucked in a corner. The houses had been built in a pine forest, which was an amazing playground. It had a sawmill and I loved to listen to the sound and it also had a quarry. We were warned to stay away but most of all there was quicksand! We had it drummed into us to stay away. We have all seen in the Westerns how horses, cattle, Indians and Cowboys disappeared in the sand never to be seen again and so we gave it a wide berth. Apart from that, it was as safe as houses to play there unsupervised.

I went to Mosstowie Primary School at the top of a hill near the monastery. On sunny days the teacher took us outside for nature study and to read us stories under the shade of a large tree. There were red spotted toadstools, just like the ones I had seen in my prize book *The Toadstool Mountain*. I could just imagine a little door in the stalk and a miniature life going on in there. We knew they were poisonous so didn't touch. A grass snake came to listen to the story but nobody was scared as we were used to seeing them.
Mum always told us never to go with strangers but I think I took it a bit far. It was heavy snow and the school was going to close early. And the teacher wanted to drive me home but I refused as I wasn't sure whether she was a stranger or not. She very kind and had to drive and collect Mum, bring her back to school and then drive us back home again. I knew she wasn't a stranger after that. I think everybody saw the funny side of it.

At school we knew the nurse and doctor were coming as our parents had to sign a consent form for the polio jab. It was a small school so we knew when the doctor arrived and we waited for the latch on the classroom door to open and the teacher picked up the register. She started at the top of the register and called out small groups of children to go with the nurse. I was already petrified and soon realised with a surname of Young, I was going to be one of the last.

There was a kettle continuously boiling to sterilise the needle. I watched children being vaccinated in their arm. When it was my turn, I watched the silver syringe and the tiny drip from the needle before the stab. The nurse kept everyone calm and it was soon over with. Everyone said it didn't hurt. And you didn't dare say otherwise. Soon after that they developed a vaccine which could be dripped onto a sugar cube and this was much more palatable.

Poliomyelitis is a crippling and potentially deadly infections disease which can invade an infected persons brain and spinal column. Many people worldwide died or were paralysed by polio. Children under 5 are the most likely to spread the disease. Vaccines became available in 1955 and the government began a programme to eradicate the disease. It has been successful in this country but lingers in Pakistan and Afghanistan. In 2013 the World Health Organisation announced an outbreak of polio in Syria. The Bill Gates Foundation is still working to eliminate the disease from the world.

Part of the heritage curriculum in Scotland is to learn and recite the poems of "Rabbie" Burns. I have no idea how Mum with her German accent managed to teach me the words of *"wee cowering timorous beastie,"* but she did. I recited it, only to be outdone by a boy called Derek. I'm convinced he won the Burns Recital Certificate because he came to school every day with his kilt on. He wore a matching tartan egg-stained tie and spat when he spoke. We did Scottish Country dancing and had to learn the sword dance. I practised at home with wooden sticks. We learned steps called "hicut" and "pah de dah." In the Highland Fling, there is lots of emphasis on finger pointing arm raising and hand positions. This is not like Irish dancing where hands and arms are kept by your sides.

One day my father came home with a bike for me. I was 8 and this was my first bike. He did it up, made it roadworthy and taught me to ride it.
At the end of the road and to the left, there was a huge downward hill with the matching upward one on the other side. I did it a few times with a mixture of riding and freewheeling and getting further and further up the other side of the hill. It was inevitable that I came a cropper. There was a huge amount of blood. Mum sat me on the

draining board to clean me up, and told me I would have a mark there for the rest of my life unless I let her. I did let her and I am still marked for life or my knee was! Fiona remembers this as well. Mum's real companion was her radio or wireless. We enjoyed Listen with Mother, always ready for the iconic start: "Are you sitting comfortably? Then I will begin." The voices of Julia Lang and Daphne Oxenford were soothing and drew us in to their storytelling.

Mum loved to sing and she joined in with any opera. I wish I could have told her that on a cruise excursion we visited Puccini's house and had a boat ride on his lake. It's only an average size house but his music was playing and the lingering smell of tobacco created an incredible atmosphere. This was a special cruise to celebrate our Silver Wedding in 1995.

She loved to listen to Mario Lanza as well as popular music of the time. Russ Conway tinkling the ivories with his beautiful teeth and smile was one of her favourites.

She always set great store by good teeth. It's hardly surprising as she had a gum disease and the dentist extracted all her beautiful top teeth. Now there is a simple cure for this. How very cruel and it made her neurotic about our teeth and we always went regularly for our check-ups. My favourite photo of Mum is one of her with a short sleeved white angora jumper, a set of pearls and her pearl like teeth. Other favourites were Doris Day and Perry Como with songs of their time like "Catch a falling star" and "Que Sera Sera."

When Fiona was about 3 she was playing with her "dungers" (dungarees)on as usual, and she was with one of the neighbour's children. They were making mud and worm pies, which you would expect, but Fiona was taking bites out of the worms as they squirmed in her mouth. It a good job they can reproduce from bits of worm and are packed with protein and mineral but she was also crunching the sand. The two children were playing a game with the spades hitting each other on the head ping pong style. Both of them were crying but neither had the sense to stop until Mum stopped them.

Mum was lonely and missed conversations in her mother tongue. Somehow she managed to get in touch with some merchant seamen from Hamburg. They were making a regular trip to Leith and visited her. Understandably she was very excited. They brought some freshly ground coffee which was not readily available here. Cafe und kuchen, the German version of afternoon tea, but an all-day version. I was playing doctors and supposedly staying out of the way. The conversation was flowing in German. Bits were familiar as Mum had taught us some words and songs. I think I stopped the conversation when I walked into the room wearing my doctor's mask, which was a sanitary towel looped around my ears. Can you imagine Mums embarrassment? At that time anything personal was very private. You went to the chemist to get sanitary towels and then they would go in a brown paper bag and any conversation was in hushed whispers. How things have changed. Before commercial "S.T.s," women just used rags, known disgustingly as "jam rags." The rags would be washed and reused which is quite unthinkable now!

Both Fiona and I had a creepy feeling about going upstairs, probably stemming from a fear of the dark. We always held our bottoms in case something got us. The first thing we did upstairs was to look under the bed. My father was hiding there and I screamed the place down. I don't know how Mum covered that one. She could not have hidden the fact that sailors were visiting. These sailors gave Mum an idea which grew in her head and soon she would act upon it.

Fochabers is close to Mosstowie and it is the home of the food manufacturer Baxter's. They were awarded the Royal warrant in the 50s as the Queen Mother was a patron. Now they are a global empire making jams, soups, chutneys, marmalades and sauces. I was impressed years later to see Ena Baxter on TV advertising their products. Local people were able earn a little extra money tattie picking. Baxter's arranged transport for the out workers and it gave people, particularly women, the chance to earn some extra money. The school holidays always coincided with the harvests and children could go with their mothers. We would get up at the crack of dawn and Mum made jam sandwiches or pieces. She spread the butter so thick you could see the teeth marks. She always used Robertson's jam, the one with the golly on, not Baxter's. The bag with the pieces in was the khaki canvas army shoulder bag which my father usually took his pieces to work in. It was all very exciting. A Land Rover collected us and took us to the field where the tractor and plough attachment turned the soil over to reveal the King Edwards. We picked the tatties and put them in the hessian sacks. At dinner time, or lunchtime depending where you lived, everyone sat by the side of the field and ate their pieces and drank the tea which tasted strange after being in the Thermos flask. At the end of the day the tractor came round and collected and weighed all the sacks and people got paid. The same thing happened when it was time to pick strawberries, raspberries and blackberries.

The biggest perk was that you could eat as much of the produce as you wanted. You had to fill the cardboard punnets right to the top or you did not get paid. It was a big surprise to me to see the range Baxter's produced in the grocers. I had not made the connection with picking the fruit and where it might end up. This is the opposite of the way most children think now. They have no idea where food comes from. My tatties could have been in a tin of Cock-a-leekie or Cullen Skink. I still smile when I see them in the supermarkets now as it was my first earned money.

Mum always referred to my father as "Buggerlugs" and it seemed as if her aversion to swearing was conquered. The name stuck and it was not a term of endearment. His life began to unravel here. There is a kind of inevitability of someone who works in a distillery becoming an alcoholic. His behaviour got worse and he was violent to Mum, but careful enough never to leave any obvious marks on her. He threw her against the sideboard and cracked several ribs and she was strapped up for ages.

One winter, when the snow was thick on the ground, Mum cut herself opening a tin of Fray Bentos bully beef. Fray Bentos is a place in Argentina with the biggest canning meat factory in the world. Mum's cut was bad and she covered her hand with a glass cloth while she took the tin up the path to the bin. There was a trail of fresh blood all the way up to the gate and all the way back and I thought Mum might bleed to death.

Buggerlugs was a good gardener and this house had a fair side plot. The trouble was he was planting empty whisky bottles in the furrows where the potatoes were growing. We came across them everywhere in the house including the airing cupboard. At the same time, he was gambling heavily on the horses and in a temper he broke the bookies window in Elgin. It was a huge plate glass window and he couldn't pay for a replacement and so his case was heard at the Sheriff Court and he was sent to prison in Inverness.

Mum was left with nothing and we had notice served on the house as my father had also lost his job. The night he went to prison Mum said her prayers and in the morning, a small miracle happened and every single sweet pea was in flower. Mum sold all the sweet peas and we were able to eat.

When he came out of prison we went to some kind of sanatorium and we visited. There were some strange people here with dressing gowns on. Mum said he was schizophrenic. I remember the word but would not have known its meaning except she always said he had two faces – one for inside the house and the other for outside. He was there for a while and we needed somewhere to live, so Mum applied to the council and being a woman on her own with two children she had little difficulty.

We were on our travels again.

Chapter 6 New Elgin. 1959-1964.

These are accurate dates from Aberdeen Archives.
New Elgin was a suburb of Elgin, although the two have now merged. It has an amazing past being created a Royal Burgh in the 12th century by King David of Scotland. It had a castle on the top of what is the present Lady Hill and it is also a former cathedral city. The ruins of the medieval cathedral are situated in Cooper Park. Sadly, it is less important now but it is still the administrative centre for Moray. At last we are somewhere near civilisation!

The first house was 68 Muirfied Road. This was a tin prefabricated house which no longer exists. These houses were built quickly and cheaply after the war to ease the housing shortage. When my father returned from his spell in clink he got himself a job which had nothing to do with distilleries. There was a chicken farm called Adams in a place just outside Elgin called Glass Green and it was here he went to work every day on his bike.

Fiona and I went to New Elgin Primary School. Initially this school was built in 1905 as a small village school. Now it has over 500 pupils and its own tartan. This was the first place that I was aware of racist remarks. Children repeat what they hear and we were "dirty rotten Nazi agents," and "jail bait." Maybe this was the root of my recurring nightmare. In my dream I am in a playground and I have only a short Cherub vest on from Woollies. No matter how hard I try I cannot cover myself and everyone is looking at me. If I pull it down at the front, more is revealed at the back but I still feel more secure with the front down and the back up. Even into my 60s I had this dream.

I suppose the rot had set in for my parents. Mum finally wrote to her father and confessed There is a saying "you make your bed and you lie in it." In this context it meant mum had married and had to stick with it. She never told her parent about her great unhappiness until now. Our lives were about to change again.

Fiona and I fought a lot, often with disastrous consequences. She used to hate the way I would wriggle out of anything with words but I was no match for her fists. I loved embroidery and used to put cross stitch motifs, mostly rabbits, everywhere but especially on my father's handkerchiefs. When I had finished sewing, I put the needle and thread into my cardigan lapel. After an argument with Fiona, she ended up with the needle in her lip. I don't know who was more shocked, but there was no real harm done.

Fiona was plagued with boils on her bottom, which I now know was a staphylococcal skin infection but Mum had a novel way of sorting it. She put Fiona over the asbestos covered ironing board and slapped a warm bread poultice on them. Fiona had to stay there for the allotted time until the poultice could come off. I had to stay with her and make sure she didn't fall off. She really suffered with the boils and at least once she had to have them lanced. Poultices are ancient natural remedies and this one was made by warming milk and then putting bread in in. The bread was squeezed and then applied while warm to draw out the pus.

The ironing board was multipurpose as the table was in the kitchen. I remember some very exciting brown paper parcels coming from Germany. They were unwrapped and carefully inspected on the ironing board. Underneath the straw there were dolls with printed faces. Germany is known for its doll making although not particularly these. All the children came to see. There were chocolate Santas and chocolate ladybirds covered in red and white foil with black paper legs and far too good to eat so they went on display. At Easter there were eggs and fluffy chicks. Everything about the package was exciting including the stamp. The asbestos may have contributed to Mums lung problems, but the dangers of asbestos were not known then. There have been cases of asbestosis which can be tracked back to ironing boards.

Uncle Gus and Auntie Mollie came to visit and they took us to Aberdeen to see Uncle Gus's friend, Bill. He had a huge house with tennis courts. We had never even imagined a house like this. Bill had a Jaguar and was obviously in a different league. I never forgot this house as it made me realise it wasn't only the Queen and Customs and Excise Officers who lived big houses.

I had fallen arches on my feet and had to go for physiotherapy at Dr

Gray's hospital. I had to put my bare feet in a basin of water with copper plates at the bottom while a current was passed through the copper plates, making my feet curl into a ball. After several sessions it did the trick and perhaps it was while she was here Mum started to think about getting a job.

The garden at the back of the house was stepped and there were always plenty of fresh vegetables. Mum's cooking was not good so even the freshest ingredients didn't help. We had curly kale and barley soup and you could stand the spoon in it, which was an acquired taste which we never acquired. The curly part of the kale never seemed to get cooked and so they would rasp your throat on the way down. Kale is seen as a super food now. Well, I don't believe it as it was used as cattle feed.

Then there was milk soup which seems to be a northern European delicacy. This was cooked macaroni with milk and sugar boiled up topped with a sprinkling of nutmeg which Mum often used. This was our sugary main meal but much better than kale soup. There was another horrid milk pudding made with sago or semolina. This was so bad we waited till Mum had gone out of the kitchen and spat it down the sink.

We liked Mum's mince, but didn't get it often. Of course she made hamburgers. The mince was mixed with chopped onions and raw egg. I loved it raw and would have gladly eaten Mr. Bean's as this is steak tartare. She also made what she called apple mousse and we call stewed apple. We had this on sandwiches with cinnamon, which sounds weird but tasty.

There are only a few recipes I copy. One of them is her delicious cabbage in white sauce with nutmeg. Mum also used a lot of caraway seeds in dishes to spice things up and make the most of cheap ingredients. There was no menu with a choice. There was nothing else so you always left a clean plate. The threat was if you didn't eat for that meal it would be in your place for the next.

Sometimes we had haggis which we loved but more often than not the haggis burst and spilled anaemically into the water and had to be fished out. The neeps and tatties were much more palatable. In Scotland neeps are swedes so the mixture was a glorious golden yellow and delicious with plenty of butter and white pepper. The spilled haggis looked like guts and in fact it is. Haggis is the national dish of Scotland and it is made of pluck, heart and liver mixed with suet and oatmeal and then encased in a sheep's stomach. Once it's stitched up it is boiled for 3 hours. Imagine all that guts swilling round in the water after it had burst. For the wimps there is a vegetarian version.

Mum's tattie patties were very good. Boiled mashed potatoes mixed with grated cheese, put in egg and then floured and pan fried. We often had Arbroath Smokies with thousands of bones. Best of all were the gloriously sticky boiled pig's trotters. The rubbery skin stuck to your fingers and had to be licked off. Mum often asked us what we wanted or dinner and our response was always the same : shit with sugar on. This was a very common response at the time.

Mum taught us to be polite and have good table manners. There was a no sapping rule! If you had food in your mouth you had to keep your mouth closed while you ate it. You always asked permission to leave the table and used the correct cutlery in the appropriate way. We even knew how to use a cake fork and a serviette.

Everyone has wind but Mum made it worse for us. When we knew we had to break wind, we had to put our bottom out the door, do the deed and then announce to everybody "pardon my bottom." It took a long time to realise if we passed wind quietly you could blame someone else just with a look for any offending odour!

On lovely days we went for walks to the local stream armed with jam jars and nets and caught sticklebacks - tiny fish with spines. We fed them with ants' eggs which is what you fed your goldfish with but now we get fancy fish flakes. We killed them with kindness as we gave them far too much food. Now we know it's not good to take fish, tadpoles, newts etc. out of their environment but then everybody did it. Newts are protected now and perhaps they were in a decline precisely because curious children captured them. You can't even build houses if there are great crested newts. Fiona was fascinated by cow pats which had dried hard on top. She watched a big beetle crawl into the pat. She put her hand in and slurped it out and put it in her pocket for the hens. You can imagine the state of her hands but a quick rub on her clothes sorted that out.

We took a small bag of dried marrowfat peas and headed out to one of the many hedgerows looking for cow parsley. The stalks were hollow inside and made fantastic pea shooters. We ate blackberries and raspberries, making sure there were no worms inside. Our mouths, fingers and clothes were all stained from the juicy experience. We picked up orange and black hairy caterpillars and were squirted with green poison as recited to them;

Little Arabella Miller
Found a furry caterpillar
First it climbed upon her mother
Then upon her baby brother
"Ugh"said Arabella Miller
"Take away that caterpillar"

Once a week we would walk to the cottages at Linkwood to have supper and watch Sports Report, a midweek sports programme with plenty of boxing. I can still hear the opening music and I hated it with good reason. Mum would tell me to go and sit on granddad's knee. Right in front of her and she couldn't see what was going on. It was one of those secrets. How apt then that his wedding certificate states he is a Groom by profession.

We learned to enjoy the boxing and I remember the names Sonny Liston and Cassius Clay who later became Muhammed Ali. His catchphrase was' "Float like a butterfly, sting like a bee. The hands can't hit what the eyes can't see."

Walking back to Muirfield Road we had to pass the high cemetery walls. It was fine when it was light but in the dark or dusk it was spine chilling. Above the walls there was a huge memorial in the shape of an obelisk and a huge hand with a finger pointing to heaven. There were huge marble angels with outstretched wings. It gave us the creeps. Fiona gripped the crossbar of my father's bike and I held Mum's hand very tightly.

My father was a good worker but there was no incremental ladder to climb where things would get better and better. It was hand to mouth, treading water but often sinking. Mum had not been back to

Germany since 1948. Her father sent her tickets to go to Hamburg and so the three of us set off on one of our greatest adventures. In Scotland a wife is owned by her husband and Mum had to get permission to take us out of the country and give an undertaking to bring us back.

We sat on the platform at Elgin station waiting for the train to Aberdeen and then to board our ship at Leith. I wondered if they were the same sailors who visited her as this was also a merchant ship which could carry a few passengers. The ship was called The Falke.

Chapter 7. Hamburg 1959

After an overnight sailing, the Falke sailed into Hamburger Harven to the strains of the German National Anthem, "Deutschland, Deutschland uber alles". The famous landmark St Pauli church, rose high above us. Only in later research did I find out that the Falke was a decommissioned A type 141 torpedo boat, built in 1894. It belonged to the German Federal Navy. Now it was a merchant vessel with a small capacity for passengers. There are pictures on the internet of the smoking room, no doubt where Mum smoked her cigs and fuelled her passion for German sailors. I remember stepping on board, eating with the crew and sleeping in a cabin. Waiting to meet us were Omi and Elfriede and I can't imagine what it must have been like for Mum to see her sister and her mother after 11 years. There was plenty of chattering in German and obvious happiness. Sadly, Hilde was not there as she was living in what was soon to become East Germany as this was the time of the Cold War with Russia.

We stayed most of the time with Elfriede and her daughter, Karen, who was "a bit slow." Elfriede's husband, Karlheinz, had been killed during the war and Rolf was his son. Elfriede now had a new partner called Heine. Mum called him hyena and didn't like him at all and he was very hairy. There were six of us sleeping in a one bedroomed flat so it was a tight squeeze. The flat overlooked a central courtyard where the children played. We quickly learned to speak German and by the time we went back home my German was quite fluent. There was no option as nobody was speaking English.

Mum began to let us go on errands to the baker for the hard morning rolls – brotchen. The shops were all so different and the sights and smells completely new. There were vending machines, the like of which I had never seen before. They sold tetra packs of pink strawberry and yellow banana milk. You put the pfennigs in the slot and the milk came down with a satisfying thump. There was a little tab on the top which pulled off and that was where the straw went in. I was fascinated and drank lots of milk.

We visited Omi, who by this time was not living with Opa. She lived in a flat in Neue ABC Strasse, (New ABC Street) which had a central courtyard mostly used by pigeons.

Again everything was different, the furniture, the ornaments, the crockery and the sound of the adults chatting. The lilt and intonation was definitely not like Scottish. Germans make a big ceremony about café und kuchen using beautiful cups, saucers and plates. Not tea sets like we had but individual settings for each person in German designs by German manufacturers. There were wonderful cakes, eaten with special cake forks and serviettes. Coffee was bought as beans and once the blend was chosen, it was put in a silver scoop, pinged into the scales and put in the bag. In her kitchen Omi had an old-fashioned grinder on the wall. The beans went in the top and you turned the handle to grind the coffee. The grounds were collected in a drawer in the bottom, and then coffee was put in a Melita filter, with paper inserts. The coffee dribbled into the pot leaving the sediment behind. I had never smelt an aroma like it or tasted such coffee and it was a very satisfying olfactory experience.

Omi believed in children being seen and not heard. I was aware of being on my best behaviour but I was never sure what to make of her. She told me,"Ich knife dich im hintern", which translates as " I'll nip you in the behind!" I never knew what I had done to warrant this threat.

A huge tasselled lampshade hung over the table where we were served. After the coffee came the cat pee wine, at least that's how it smelt. It was Liebfraumilch, which I never liked, or any other German wine. We wanted Pepsi. Omi took a piece of beef and put it in a glass which she filled the with Pepsi and told us, the next time we came the meat would be gone because the Pepsi would have eaten it. That's what it would do to our stomachs she said. Three days later the meat was gone so either it was true or she fished it out. It was gruesome but it didn't put me off.

Everywhere we went there were net curtains. Ours were put on wires but these were beautiful drapes that had proper tape on the top. They even had rods to pull them open and closed. They were fashionable for many years and are typically Germanic and nobody had them in Elgin but they soon would.

On one trip to Omi, we met Hubert who was in his late teens or early 20s. I never thought anything of it at the time but I remember great secrecy surrounding him. He was Hilde's son and he had escaped from the East to the West. Hubert was eventually killed on what was known as The Death Line crossing the Berlin Wall.

We stayed for some of the time with Opa and his new partner, whom we called Tante Elsa. She had a daughter called Inge who was about five years older than me. She was fantastic and we had good fun with her. She played with us and was really friendly. Her hair was done in a top not with an elastic band and had a fountain spray of hair sticking out the top which was very trendy.

Mum took us to a huge shop called Karstad. Her father must have given her some money as we were kitted out in new clothes. We both had the traditional costume of the Deutsche madchen which consisted of a gypsy type embroidered blouse and a denim dirndl skirt with a bib front and crossed straps at the back. We were thrilled to bits but I'm glad we weren't boy's as I didn't fancy the lederhosen. They look particularly stupid on grown men, but now they are worn mostly for beer festivals and I suppose they drink so many steins of Holsten they are beyond embarrassment.
 We also had a growling Herman teddy each and a doll. I called mine Jotta and Fiona called hers Inge. Germans were known for their toys and I still have my Hermann bear but like me, he has lost his growl.
One day we went to visit Mum's friend Lotte. She lived in a bungalow with a garden. It was a hot day and we must have gone prepared for paddling. I had a blue swimming costume with shirring elastic all the way round. It only served to make my belly look bigger so nothing has changed. I had my photo taken cooling myself with a watering can. Lotte had a giant tortoise which was older than our great grandmother and it was big enough to ride on.

We were spoiled with gifts. Elfriede gave us both a "betein kette," or begging chain. It was just a silver necklace but the tradition was that anyone who touched it had to buy you a silver charm to put on it. Everyone knew about it so you wouldn't touch it if you didn't want to contribute. We both ended up with three charms. I chose a penguin, a greyhound and an angel. I added to the charms when I got older and If remember going to buy them in the jewellers. There were trays full of silver delights. A miniature of every object you could think of. In the 60s and 70s charm bracelets became popular in either silver or gold. I had so many charms the necklace became heavy and I had it converted to a bracelet. It caught on everything and was given the name clinker because of the noise it made when I was wearing it. In the end there were 65 charms reflecting my love of animals and birds. There were shield shaped charms from travels to Germany, Hamburg, Berlin, Blankenese, from Spain, Tossa de Mar, Lloret de Mar, Barcelona, Blanes, san Felou de Guixols, Monserrat and Gerona. There was a dachshund, a German weather station with a moveable man and lady and a Hummel Hummel. This is a traditional Hamburger greeting. Hummel was a water carrier who carried water through the streets in double buckets suspended from a yoke around his shoulders. The children would run behind him shouting Hummel Hummel. He would get annoyed and answer back "Mors, mors," meaning "Arse, arse." As Mum could never say arse it was always arsh, arsh and that is how we learned it! Other charms included Big Ben, Saint Paul's Cathedral and Blackpool Tower. Other sundry items included an opening apple with Adam and Eve inside, a heart shaped opening box with a solitaire ring inside, an opening telephone with the emergency numbers inside and a teapot with an opening lid.

I did keep clinker as it had many happy memories for me. There were no lobster claw fastenings then and each charm had to be individually soldered on which was a pain and expensive. Eventually I gave it to my daughter Grace and she has designs on modernising and streamlining it by picking her favourites. I had years of fun and interest from my begging chain.

Fiona had hair like an angel. She often had it in plaits but now mum made her look like Heidi with them wrapped round her ears. Fiona was like the incredible sulk when she wasn't happy! She definitely wasn't happy when mum bought her a bun ring for her hair. She had to have her hair brushed right up on the very top of her head and tied with an elastic. Then her hair was pulled through a bun ring and clips put in to make it tidy. It was eye watering for Fiona. They call that some kind of facelift now.

Mum had her box Brownie with her but she took us to a photo booth to have photos done. Fiona and I are side by side in identical clothing and bears, me smiling and Fiona with her trademark sulk. It's there for posterity and she can't deny it!

Opa smoked cigars and eventually he died of lung cancer. He was kind enough to us while we were there but we didn't see him often and don't remember any affection. Mum did tell us he was active in the underground movement helping British soldiers. We went to Luneburg to see our paternal great grandmother. She was tiny, old and dressed in black as my great grandfather had died years before. It was a lovely day when we visited and she was sitting outside on a chair. She had what Roald Dahl would have described as a dog's bottom for a mouth as she had no teeth and her gums had sunken in. She also had the smell of really ancient people.

Luneburg was memorable and is now a World Heritage site. The buildings are unusual but what fascinated me were the storks. They make spiky stick nests in chimney pots and they are everywhere, or they were when we visited. Every year they make this amazing repetitive journey, covering exactly the same route. I had no idea then that this is a famous German stork route "Deutche Storchenstrasse" Stork Street which travels through Germany for 450 kilometres of natural landscape, mostly following the Elbe. There are over 100 towns villages and hamlets where the storks nest and there are storks signs for the tourists to follow. We were there in August when lots of the gangly baby storks were leaving their nests. We were told that these were the storks that bring the babies. There were lots of storks and lots of babies so very believable.

From Victorian times it has been popular for children to collect scraps and paste them in their scrapbook. The Germans were particularly good at producing these. I mention it here because my favourite scrap was a stork holding a baby in a blanket, and best of all it had glitter on. The scraps were wonderful, children, people from many lands, animals, Santas with bulging sacks, fairy stories, fairies with flower hats, pixies, spotted toadstools, angels, cupids, flowers, all joined with tabs easily released with one snip of the scissors, manageable for little fingers. Many of the scraps had the same look as Mum's treasured Hummel figurines, a boy with a top hat blowing a clarinet, a girl tending her deer, a girl with pigtails flying out behind her, all a bit twee for today's market but fashionable and valued at the time.

Luneburg is also famous for its heath with the beautiful heather. Visiting as an adult the city has some beautiful architecture. What really surprised us though was to see special places for women to park. Easy parking spots – ahem!!

Rolf, my lovely older cousin was 18 and I was 9. He took me to the Star Club in Hamburg where the Beatles had just played. I was already a massive fan so it was very exciting and grown up. He also let me have my very first sneaky puff of a cigarette.

We went to one of the famous funfairs. It was dark and the lights were mesmerising. The colours and rides were wonderful. We both got a gingerbread spiced heart(Lebkuchenherzen) to hang around our necks with our names piped on them. Then there was the aroma of the tantalising range of sausages. When the German market came to Manchester it brought back the most wonderful memories. We learned the wonders of German cuisine. Die wurst! (sausages) Bratwurst, Bockwurst, Teewurst, Knackwurst, Fleishwurst, Bierwurst, salamis, Mettwurst and Mums favourite liverwurst or liver sausage. This was spreadable often on black pumpernickel with Lurpak slightly salted butter.
Germans do not have sandwiches like we do, they have open sandwiches and the bread filling could be prawns with Hellmann's mayonnaise and a topping of caviar – not beluga but lumpfish caviar. Hellmann's was invented by the wife of a German in New York in 1905 and no self-respecting German would dream of using any other brand. There were frankfurters from Frankfurt and hamburgers from Hamburg and all served with the same pale yellow "senf" or mustard. Sausages were often accompanied with kartofel (potato) salad made with lots of Hellmann's, or sauerkraut mixed with caraway seeds. Or hot sweet, roht kohl (red cabbage) with apples and cloves or hot white cabbage served in a white sauce with lots of butter and nutmeg. They have a lovely cucumber salad made with thinly sliced cucumber, sugar, white wine vinegar and fresh dill. Breaded veal, Wiener schnitzel or fried breaded fish are also popular in a bun. Smoked eel from the Elbe is a great delicacy. Rolf laughed

when my husband Barry said they were snakes – his great fear!

Germany relies heavily on its fish from the wonderful fish market. Herring is plentiful and made into rollmops. We often had whitebait which mum would relish, these are little immature fish covered on flour and deep fried and eaten whole. On one return visit as adults, the three of us went to the fish market in Hamburg. It's a wonderful place which opens before five in the morning and is in a giant hanger. Rock bands perform whist the fish were being sold outside! It was freezing. Fiona had nothing on her feet under her boots and had to try to find heaters to warm them. This is a really memorable place with wonderful food mostly with fried potatoes, onions and fish.

The Germans like the sour taste and this includes gherkins – sauer gurken. Mums preferred brand was the Polish Krakus for rollmops, sauerkraut and red cabbage. Germany borders Netherlands, Belgium, Switzerland, Austria, Czech Republic and Poland and therefore the culinary delights are influenced by this. Altona, the district of Hamburg where Elfriede lived was in fact Danish until 1864
The café und kuchen were served everywhere we visited. There were lots of tortes but I don't remember schwarzwalder kirchtorte, (black Forest gateau) Apples were used in many of the cakes and I loved apple strudel. Each individual place was set with a side plate for the cake and there was always a serviette. Everybody was very proud of their cups and saucers. Along with the eggshell thin Chinese import sets, I have Mitterteich from, Shrinding, Alboth and Keiser, Zeh Scherzer all from what was Bavaria, which is a state in the south east of Germany. Then the grown-ups had wine at every opportunity. Mum would always choose Holsten lager out of a stein if she could. If there were pretzels around so much the better. It was usually later in the day when the Jägermeister or the schnapps came out. There was a drink called Underberg, a digestive remedy made from the herbs of 43 different countries and the recipe is still an Underberg family secret. Maybe after all that alcohol you needed something to settle your stomach.

Mum did make a fabulous punch. In a punch bowl she put a couple of bottles of sparkling wine called Verve de Verney. Then she took peaches and pierced them all over with a fork and put them in the bowl and magically they spun and spun. Then they were ladled into the punch cups. Mum made this till she was into her 70's.

Mum loved cheese, the hard geska cheese I mentioned before. The smellier the cheese the better, Danish Blue, Gorgonzola, Emmental and Leerdammer mouse cheese with holes in.

She also had a lifelong obsession with salmiakpastillen. These were diamond shaped lozenges made with liquorice root extract, ammonium chloride and anise oil. They were not sweets. The ammonium chloride was a traditionally administered drug to help the mucus in the respiratory tract. The word salmi is short for diamond. She would have loved to be able to order on line instead of relying on other people to get them for her. Every time she emptied her handbag there were decaying salmies stuck to the lining.

The children here had the most fabulous wicker dolls prams. These were produced in Warlsdorf which was the centre of the German wicker industry from 1955, so when we were there they were the latest fashion. It was an object of envy for any little girl. Fiona and I never got one but years later Fiona's daughter Louise was thrilled to receive a mini version which mum dragged back from Hamburg.

Two German fragrances make me think of Mum and Omi. Firstly, there is the perfume Tosca and then 4711 toilet water which was an Eau de Cologne, or water from Cologne – echt kolnishwasser. They were in so called Molanus bottle or watch bottle. Every time mum came back from a holiday she would bring some 4711 for us. Long before we had any kind of wipes 4711 had them and they are magic for freshening up when travelling. Mum always had some and the solid cologne stick which was excellent for cooling when applied to the inner elbows, wrists and forehead and good for headaches when applied to the temples.

Oddly during WW2 vast amounts of 4711 were given to submariners of the U-boat fleet as there were not many opportunities for bathing. It was an attempt to improve the odour on board the vessel. However most of it was never used and went back home for female relatives.
4711 is still popular today. Even the Queen Mother liked it. When

we visited the Castle of Mey I was amused to see a bottle in one of the bathrooms.

We were taken to a Park called Planten un Blomen which literally means plants and flowers. There were playgrounds, pony rides and a roller skating rink. There were nightly water and light concerts and it was an early forerunner of the Bellagio Hotel in Las Vegas. There were tame red squirrel's eager to take nuts from your hand. They have lovely tufty ears and are smaller than their grey cousins. There were water lilies the size of dinner plates with a frilled lip around the edge. Big enough to hold a sleeping baby.

We have made a return visit to see Rolf who lives in Schleswig Holstein on the banks of Ratzeburg Lake and where the British zone was. Back to Lubeck to the home of Mums beloved Niederegger marzipan, to the factory for café and kuchen with Monika Rolf's wife, back to Luneburg and Bremen with fried fish and steak tartare sandwiches.

Rolf took us to Travemunde which is Germany's oldest seaside resort. Here on the beach they have the famous Strandcorb which literally means "basket chair." They are made from wicker with two seats. The tops are tilt able so people could either lie back or lie down. They have armrests, footrests and storage underneath. They also have rainproof covers and sunshades. You hire them like we hire deckchairs. Travemunde and the Strandcorbe can be seen on Google Earth. There is a better home version for the garden. They are still hand woven and expensive.

We couldn't stop sniggering because we went on a Harfen rundfart. Just a trip round the harbour but to see the word fart written everywhere was deliciously wicked. We assumed most Germans would not know the English version. As we went round the shipyard I couldn't help wondering if my Opa had worked there. As an adult Barry and I went on a cruise on a Fred Olsen ship called the Balmoral. I was amazed to find out that the ship had been extended. It had literally been cut in two. A new centre piece had been prefabricated and then welded back in and all in Hamburger Harfen shipyard. We inspected the joins carefully but the Balmoral was sea worthy. Apparently this is common practise. What would Opa have made of that!

In Hamburg we saw for the first time the little green and red man crossings. We wanted to cross roads all day and it was years before I saw another one.

We were taken to Hagenbeck's zoo and we had never been to a zoo before. It was amazing. We had a ride on a pony which was another first. I particularly liked the big cats, giraffes and elephants.

Eventually of course we had to go back to Bonnie Scotland. Inge gave me an oversized pale blue needle cord coat. It was so big I had to fold the cuffs back, but I felt years older than the nine-year-old who left Scotland. I had had a taste of life in a big city and I liked what I saw.

There were plenty of tears as we left again on the Falke. Things would never be the same again.

Chapter 8   12 Muirfield Road

Back to 12 Muirfield Road, New Elgin, where we lived from 1960-1964.
I was aged 10 and Fiona aged 6.

We stayed a few more months in 68 but Mum never liked the tin house and was constantly badgering the council for a move. When it finally came she was impressed as the previous tenant was a council official.
The trip to Germany had given her a new impetus to do up the house. It was still only a small two bedroomed house but with the permanence of brick and the air of a former tenant which gave kudos with her neighbours.
Mum got a job as an Auxiliary Nurse at Dr. Grey's hospital on Pluscarden Road. It is the smallest District Hospital in Scotland with 185 beds. Not happy with one job, she cleaned for the kilt makers Mr. and Mrs. Munroe. During the school holidays we were allowed to go with her. They were lovely friendly people and made us feel most welcome. There were shelves stuffed with bolts of every tartan available: Anderson, Black Watch, Cameron, Campbell, Frazer, Gordon, Macdonald, Macfarlane, Mackenzie, MacLeod, Morrison and Stewart. My favourite was Blue Douglas. Handmade kilts are very expensive as they are still handwoven but they last a lifetime. Most people had a lookey-likey version and the tartan was usually Royal Stewart. It is true that Scotsmen don't wear anything under their kilts. It is even a battle cry when soldiers run out of ammunition, "kilts up, cocks out, charge!" The money started coming in and Mum had a measure of financial independence. She would never divulge to my father how much she had as he would drink or gamble it.

The house had a big back garden and a further piece of land the whole length of the house. Buggerlugs cycled to work every day with his piece bag across his body.
My father built a huge chicken coop at the back of the house and he got some pullets from the farm. They were Rhode Island Reds which are known for being good layers. We loved having the chickens and

our favourite was Jennie who we dug up worms for her. As my son Danny found out from his experiences, hens attract little red spiders which got everywhere. We wouldn't sit on walls or fences as we believed they stung.

Perhaps it was the hens that drew other pests into the house. Moths permeated every fabric as they were all natural and so you had to put mothballs in every wardrobe. They look like mint balls but have a very distinctive smell. They were made of naphthalene, which gave off a gas, killing the moths and the larvae. In the living room, hanging from the ceiling or the lampshade, was the flycatcher, a sticky ringlet of brown paper. You waited until it was full of decayed and dehydrated flies before you replaced it. The new one was a long roll of the sticky stuff which you had to pull out from the middle and it often stuck to skin and clothes. The paper is impregnated with pheromones to entice the flies to their sticky death. It's not exactly nice having this fly paper with maybe 100 assorted flies dangling up above and blowing in the wind. We had mouse traps under the sink and a cat but there were so many mice he couldn't eat them all.

At Dr. Grey's, Mum had to wear a lavender-coloured uniform, white cap and starched apron and elasticated belt with a big silver buckle. It didn't look like my Mum. She absolutely loved the job and had a great respect and admiration for the doctors and nurses who worked there. She moved about the hospital group to Spynie and Bilbohall. One of these was the mental hospital. She told us about patients who threw poo and at least once Mum got some stuck in her hair. The saddest story was about a journalist who died after a parachute accident. I know it upset her and she tried hard not to show it but we heard that part of the metal went right through his head. It must have been hard for Mum to nurse him.

She had to go to work on her bike. It was often icy and cold so she wore flesh pink, knee length winceyette knickers, elasticated at the knee to keep the cold out. Mum had a good sense of fun and enjoyed freewheeling down the hill with her legs in the air showing off her knickers to all and sundry. She had the odd tumble off her bike here when it was icy but she took it in her stride.

We had plenty of eggs from the pullets. So many we got sick of them and Mum had to invent ways of using them. She made a drink with eggs, milk and sugar which she whisked, and we had to drink it because it was good for us. It did not slide well down the throat. Often the albumen was in gloopy chunks and it made us heave. Sometimes you even had to hold your nose and swallow. The chickens were food when they stopped laying. My father would wring their necks, pluck them and use his lighter to singe the feather ends. Mum had to prepare the bird for the oven and we watched. She put her hand up the chicken and pulled all the inside out. She showed us the heart, lungs and liver. There were still oats in the crop and underdeveloped eggs in the tract. Mum cut off the feet and pulled the tendons which made the foot move and we were experiencing first hand learning.

I didn't have a good relationship with my father and I remember the day I started calling him names. I only called him Mustard Face but perhaps I said it once too often. He chased me upstairs and I managed to get to the bathroom and lock the door. He got madder and madder and tried to break the door down. I put my feet on the back of the door and wedged my back on the cistern. I was terrified. The banging went on for a long time and I could feel the door giving way. At the bottom of the stairs was the locked gun cabinet. Everything went quiet and I thought he was going to shoot me. Fiona was playing and Mum was at work. I was frozen to the spot for a long time. I tentatively opened the door expecting him to be there but he wasn't. I went downstairs and checked the gun cabinet and was glad to see both guns were there. I looked round the living room door and he seemed to have gone. I got my purse and went to the phone box on the corner. I lifted the receiver, put in my four pennies and dialled the hospital. When it was answered I pressed the button and the coins fell down. I left a message for Mum asking her to come home and she did. I think this was the last straw.

Mum began to look in the Situation Vacant columns for a job. There was an eerie calm in the house, a kind of vacuum where you felt something was happening but didn't know what. She looked in the Daily Express and The Lady magazine for a job as a housekeeper where children were welcome. She collected the replies from a Post Office Box. Maybe she conducted some kind of interview on the phone with hundreds of old pennies. I don't know, but I do know nothing would have come to the house and Mum would never have trusted any of the neighbours. Whatever happened, we were packing again.

Chapter 9 Halkirk Caithness

February and March 1961.

We left Elgin Station on the way to Inverness where we had to change trains. Outside Inverness Station there is a magnificent statue of a piper on a raised plinth and it was here we stayed the night. The hotel had a beautiful wooden staircase which split into two at the top. This was a very special occasion for us.

The journey to Halkirk on the Far North Line was incredible. A cushioned quilt of thick snow covered the landscape. There were enormous mountains on either side of glens where the clever Victorians had managed to build railway lines running parallel to the road. This is a wild magnificent place where Golden Eagles and peregrine falcons fly. It is a wild and austere wonderland, and one of the most sparsely populated places in Europe.

Mum started her job as a housekeeper in this, a village on the river Thurso in Caithness. We arrived at Georgemas station. Had we been a few months earlier we could have got off at Halkirk station which closed as part of the Beeching cuts in 1960. Halkirk station was within walking distance of the house where we stayed. We had been plucked from Elgin and deposited here in the middle of the winter, to a bungalow called Loos Cottage. The first people to own the house named it after their son who was killed at the battle of Loos which took place in 1915.

The bungalow was warm and welcoming as was Mum's new employer, Willie Mathieson and his brother. Our stay here was brief but memorable.

The snow was wonderful, and there was a swing in the garden which we loved. Behind the house there was nothing except mountains and flat lands, where the grass grew sideways due to the exposure to the wind. It was a place where we could be wild and free. In the far distance we could see the sea and the Dounreay Nuclear Reactor which became active in 1958. From where we were it looked like a giant ping pong ball. There was something really spooky and alien about it and it has since been dismantled.

We collected plover's eggs which Willie told us were a delicacy.

Whatever you want to call them – plovers, lapwings or peewits- it's all the same. They are ground nesting and wading birds with a distinctive peewit call, iridescent plumage and a magnificent crest on their head. Mum cooked the quail-sized eggs and we ate them with glee, although there was no difference in taste to the hen's eggs. There were oyster catchers with long orange legs and beaks and curlews with their curled beaks poking for worms in the scrubby land.

It was lambing time and the snow was thawing. Sheep roamed freely, sheltering from the easterly wind in the ruins of outbuildings. We watched a sheep give birth. Fiona ran back to Mum shouting, "Mammy, Mammy, the sheep has pooped a lammy and it still in the bag." This was absolutely priceless and never to be forgotten. We still talk about it now.

Mum had to send us to school and, as there was only Halkirk Primary, there was no choice. This is now a non-denominational school but then was Catholic. For the first time in our lives we had to walk to the end of the road to get the school bus. The school was fine and we soon made friends. The only thing we were not used to was the worship. We had to learn to chant from a little book with a brown cover and it was called the catechism. It had a question and answer format teaching the doctrine for Catholicism. For example, "Who made you?" Answer: "God." "What else did God make?" "God made all things." "Why did God make you and all things?" "For his own glory." In all there are 145 questions and answers in increasing complexity. Even then I never understood its relevance other than indoctrination.

I think Mum was fairly happy here and people were welcoming. Willie and his brother were kind to us. They must have already had or acquired a sewing machine and they encouraged Mum to take in alterations. One of the teachers from the school came to have a skirt made and another altered. I remember her standing in her petticoat whilst mum measured her. It was very unusual to see a figure of authority in her scanties. She had a heavy Harris Tweed cloth wrapped in brown paper. Oddly it smelt very strongly of pepper.

Mum arranged a small party for my 11th birthday on March 28th.

Mum's food was always different because of her German heritage. She knew a lot about etiquette and must have moved in sophisticated circles. We invited six girls from my class but I can only remember the name Wanda as it seemed so exotic. She gave me a little wooden mouse with leather ears and tail which I kept for 30 years. Willie and his brother bought me a box of embroidered hankies which was a normal gift to give in the days before tissues in this country.

What was on the menu for the party? Halved boiled eggs, with the yolks mashed with mayonnaise and topped with an anchovy. I had no idea anchovies were not part of a normal child's diet in Halkirk but there were quite a few left over. Of course there were the usual jellies and sandwiches as well.

As a child I often saw the show of the Northern Lights or the Aurora Borealis, the natural light display but here they were the most spectacular.

I revisited Halkirk in 2012. I had found Loos cottage on Google earth and it was still as I remembered with no new houses and the railway line at the end of the road. Halkirk lies about half way between Wick and Thurso. At the time I had no idea how close we were to the castle of Mey. Now I can imagine my contemporary Prince Charles, in the castle with his Granny the Queen Mother who he adored. Scrabster is close by and this is where the Royal Yacht Britannia would moor when the family visited. It seems like a place where there was lots of fun. On the top of one of the paintings in the castle there is a toy Nessie (Loch Ness Monster.) Apparently, the Queen Mother liked to move it around, much to the annoyance of her Lady-in-Waiting. When the visiting party left, the royal family on the boat would sail from Scrabster, past the castle and they would have a firework competition to see who had the biggest, loudest fireworks. In the hallway of the castle there is still the coat and wellies which she wore. She was another royal who was economical with her clothes and wore the same thing many times. The castle is modest and not at all stuffy.

Neither did I know how close we were to John O Groats. Recently we visited and the weather was idyllic with views over to the Orkneys and Cape Wrath which were nothing short of incredible. The rock formation at the Dunnet head bird sanctuary reminds me of Vietnam with pointed needles coming out of the sea. I had a "David Attenborough" moment looking down the cliffs at the fulmars and the rock plants we have now in our rockery gardens.

Scotland is all the more beautiful to return to in magnificent sunshine. We were travelling in the back of a car with a glass sunroof which was ideal for a spot of snow-capped mountain gazing from the back seat. We travelled on the A836 through the National park. We made a sudden stop to see a herd of red deer sitting motionless staring at us. It was magical.

Three days after my birthday we left Halkirk. Whatever you call it, rumbling or grumbling appendicitis, mine had been getting worse and the bouts of pain lasting longer and longer. Mum was worried it would burst. We were in the middle of nowhere and she had visions of me being helicoptered out. The helicopter would have had to come from Lossiemouth and this would have taken a dangerously long time. This was at a time when there was no such thing as the air ambulance. Mum made the decision to return to Elgin so I could have an appendectomy. Her children always came first. It's just a good job she didn't know what Willies brother had been up to.

Like Robert the Bruce, she decided *"if at first you don't succeed, try, try and try again."*

Chapter 10 Return to Elgin.

It was as if we had never been away and nothing was said as Mum picked up her jobs again. I had no idea what my father thought. I was expecting him to be angry or hostile, but as far as we could see, there was no difference. There was always a thing, even in a violent and failing marriage, that couples should staying together for the children but it's not something I would subscribe to.

We went back to school and apart from the jibes I loved it and I remember all the classrooms. There was one teacher who I particularly liked and I remember where I sat in the classroom. I learned my left from my right here. Even now I sometimes flash back to the classroom to remember that my right hand is the one near the window. What an admission, but I know now I am not alone in this.

I was a good reader but still didn't like it when we read a book right round the class. Panic set in as you started to figure out which bit you would be reading. You knew who the good and bad readers were and you cringed for the ones who got stuck or lost their place. The worst bit was, you always had to finish the sentence so, it would mean turning the page over and then the next person had to find the beginning of the next one.

I enjoyed the daily story we had, and in particular, The Wind in the Willows so, I was delighted when this was one of my Christmas presents. Books were expensive and were normally only given on special occasions. Miss Maine hated when people turned over the corner of pages to mark their place, "Books are our friends," she would say, "don't bend their ears." She did the most interesting Nature Study lessons and I was always looking for pictures to cut out from my Knowledge magazine to put in my nature study book. We had a nature table and went for walks to collect twigs from different trees, so we could learn to identify them by leaf or bud. Miss Maine left at the end of the year to get married and go and live in Saltash in Cornwall. I thought about her for a long time after she left.

The next year I was on the other side of the hall. Mr. Mackay was the headmaster and he appeared from time to time mostly to take assemblies. He stood at the front of the hall and behind him was a wooden roll call board of the Head Boy and Girl. I was NOT head girl material. I wasn't happy in this new class and was often in trouble. I was constantly swinging on my chair legs usually with my thumbs under my gym slip straps. Then there was the maths. I had no problem learning my tables but just like reading round the class I panicked when it came to tests. Mental arithmetic problems were a nightmare for me. The sort that start with something like "how long did it take the train to get from A to B travelling at 50 miles per hour with three stops of 15 minutes' duration." I never heard the end of the question nor the one after that which I could have answered! The result was that I always got full marks in spelling tests and very poor ones in mental arithmetic, so, I copied. Probably once too often. The girl I copied from and myself at the age of nine got the three fingered strap or taws across the hand. My maths never recovered, until I myself had to teach and learn at the same time. The result was, I was much more sympathetic with my pupils. I remember the weekly spelling test and always learned them for home work. One or two were problematic for me to learn. I remember having difficulty with the word station. I chanted the letter names STATION what seemed like a hundred times. Every time I got ten out of ten I got sixpence. Needless to say I never got ten out of ten for mental arithmetic.

The next class was Miss Cuthbert's I hated her from the word go. She had long red fingernails and a long nose and looked very witchy. She had her own cruel ways of punishing children. She would bend her finger and poke you several times in the top of your arm. Nobody said anything about bruises then. You didn't get a choice but the alternative was just as bad. A ruler sideways across the knuckles. I was subjected to both and as a result anything I learned was out of fear. Again it was mental arithmetic which crippled me. She walked up and down the rows watching you working and the minute you got a wrong answer you got the knuckle or the ruler. This was nothing short of Dickensian. We met her once on a train and she was as "nice as ninepence." She was the worst teacher I ever had – bar none. Nowadays this would be both assault and gross misconduct resulting in dismissal but really was the norm in a time when corporal punishment was quite acceptable.

My last year at the primary school was much happier. We did handicrafts, which I looked forward to every Friday afternoon. I had always loved to knit, sew and embroider. We learned to knit a scarf and had to take it home for homework. It was Royal blue with a ribbed central panel. We were shown how to knit the Scottish way, but Mum could only knit the continental way with the wool wrapped round her index finger. This is how I knit now but trying to learn the two methods and being told at school that I was doing it the wrong way was confusing, but I finished it and wore it.

We made a purple raffia basket with a lid, and an embroidered pencil case. We learned back, running, feather, stem, whipped and herringbone stitches. Herringbone was the one Mum always used for hems, so it was a really useful one to learn. Embroidery for young ladies is seen a relic from times gone by when it was a necessary female attribute. I was amused to see it is having a resurgence. When we had finished the embroidery, the pencil case had to be lined with satin. As part of this exercise required pinning the satin to the canvas, I had the novel idea of putting the pins between my lips in preparation. I sneezed and swallowed all the pins on the intake breath. Mum was sent for and I had to go to Dr. Grey's hospital for an x-ray. They could see all the pins and they were all facing in the right direction for a safe exit. I was sent home and told to eat dry bread. Mum was told to prepare the newspaper and a safe passage occurred the next day.

The boys went off with Mr. Mackay to do woodwork, a kind of sexist segregation that was seen as the norm.

I only remember one school trip to the small seaside resort of Buckie. We went on a charabanc, all carrying our metal buckets and spades. It is not far from Elgin to Buckie and the journey was memorable and exciting. We rose to the top of the hill and looked down at the sea. It was the first time I had been to the seaside to play. We made a few sandcastles and had our picnic before returning. It's hard to imagine now, but that was the holiday for the whole year.

Sometimes I went to stay at Linkwood. Granny made the best scrambled eggs I have ever tasted. They were golden yellow, fluffy eggs with a lovely buttery taste. I played in the back garden and went down to the bottom where the trains rumbled past. The toilet was outside and the toilet paper was Izal which is like tracing paper, and that's what we used it for. The seat was a wooden square lid with a central hole. I don't know why I had to stay at Granny's but if Mum knew what was happening she would never have let it.

We often went on bike rides and we rode to fields where we knew there were sheep and pulled off all the wool from the barbed wire, collecting it in a bag. We brought it home, washed it, and filled dolls quilts and pillowcases with it using it as a stuffing.

Mum was proud and resourceful. We seldom had new clothes. She would go an extra stop on the bus to be sure that the jumble sale clothes she bought did not belong to any of the neighbours. We had a pair of tartan trews each. They must have been proper tartan because they chafed until our legs were red raw. Mum had to make linings for both of us from pillowcases. She brought back jumpers. Sometimes they fitted, sometimes they were huge, but she had deliberately bought them like that. They were for unpicking. This was a laborious task involving each garment being unpicked to reveal its component parts – sleeves, front and back. Each individual piece was unpicked and rolled back into balls before re-knitting into another garment. We never liked wearing the jumble sale clothes but what else could Mum do? There is a famous cashmere factory called Johnstone's of Elgin. It's a shame no cashmere jumpers turned up but then Mum would probably have shrunk them to doll size!

Parcels continued to arrive from Germany for Christmas and Easter, and it was always very exciting. We got dolls one Christmas, and chocolate Santas. At Easter we received eggs and cards which were like postcards saying Froe Ostern. Mum made Easter special by hiding the eggs and chickens all over the house. We both had little baskets to collect them in. There was a bit of engineering so that we both had a similar amount of eggs. She would tell us when we were "warm, cold or very hot." Like everybody else we boiled eggs and decorated them. There were no felts then, so they had to be painted or stained while cooking, using things like onion skins and cochineal in the water. Cochineal is a scarlet food dye made from the crushed dried bodies of the female scale insect which is native to Mexico. Now a synthetic dye is used, thank goodness.

All the local children collected on a hill on Easter Sunday and rolled our eggs down to the bottom. If the weather was nice we had a picnic of jam sandwiches, which were wrapped in greaseproof paper, and there was a flask of very sweet tea to keep us warm.

Mum was good at knitting in her German style with the wool wrapped round her finger. Wool came mostly in hanks rather than balls, as this was much cheaper. The hanks had to be untwisted and rolled into balls, so we put the hanks on our outstretched arms whilst Mum rolled them into balls. We had to tilt our arms from one side to the other to allow the free flow of wool. By the time all the hanks were done you had real arm ache. You could put the hank on the back of the chair and wind from there, but it invariably went into unforgiving knots which would mean a break in the wool and a telling off.

The most exciting time of year for us was Christmas, but not generally in Scotland. At the time of John Knox in 1580, it was seen to be papist in origin and was banned by law. It was not even a public holiday until 1958, so people would go to work as normal before this. The children did get presents but it was very low key. Hogmanay or New Year's Eve is still the main celebration. I keep promising myself to go to Edinburgh for the Hogmanay celebrations and watch the haggis being piped in. I remember Mum always wanted someone to do the "first footing." This was a custom when you welcomed in the New Year with the first person who crossed the threshold, who was believed to be the bringer of good fortune for the rest of the year. Ideally the person would bring a piece of coal and be tall, dark and handsome. I do remember being awake for the pre-arranged activity a couple of times. You had to be sure someone would come and knock on the door at midnight. It didn't count if they were there before. You couldn't for example, go out the back door and come back in the front. At the stroke of 12 everybody in the house would link arms and sing, "Auld Lang Syne", which was another gem from Rabbie Burns. Copious amounts of single malt were consumed and there were many sore "heeds" the next day.

I do remember one Christmas party we went to in Elgin, which was actually in the New Year. We had to bring our own plate and spoon. The plate was for the "sangwiches," and the spoon was for the trifle which was served in the traditional waxed paper containers with fluted edges. Every child got a present from Santa and there seemed to be every child in Elgin in attendance.

Christmas in our house was the full blown celebration. We were one of the few houses to have a real Christmas tree with glass decorations and real candles on clips. Mum would sing "Oh Tannenbaum" to us. The tree had tinsel, silver lametta and wavy angel's hair. We lit the candles for a little while every night, but due to the fire hazard it was brief and we gave it our full attention, drawn in by the spectacle. The candles had a kind of aura around them and the smell was lovely. After we had left carrots for the reindeer and a drink of whisky for Santa, we went excitedly to bed and waited. One of the ornaments was a trumpet which did make a sound. Every Christmas, Santa blew the trumpet when he had been and we knew not to move a muscle! Most of the ornaments had been sent from Germany. I know, in Windsor Castle, Prince Albert had sorted a huge tree for Queen Victoria since 1840, because of course, he was German and it was Albert who started the tradition in this country. When I look at photos of our early trees they were not quite the symmetrical beauties I remember! Nevertheless, they were magical Christmases.

"Weinachten" in Germany is started with the opening of gifts on Christmas Eve. I loved the paper advent calendar which Fiona and I took it in turns to open. It was a lovely surprise to see what was behind each door or window. Now, with the Christmas markets and, pardon the pun, the advent of Aldi and Lidl the magic seems diluted.

Mum always was terrified of thunder and lightning. At the first rumble she would open a window – to let the lightening out if it got in. Everything electrical was turned off. She kept blankets to cover the mirrors and all shiny items, including cutlery, had to be hidden. When all the preparation was complete we retreated under the dining room table. After the storm a candle was lit and Mum would go searching for any scorch marks the lightening might have left. We had to stay under the table until the coast was clear. She never got over this fear.

Eventually, a letter came from the hospital saying I had to go in for an appendectomy. They put me in a mixed ward with old men and a lady in the next bed called Mrs. Mallet. She was an old windbag and she farted all day and all night and the farts ricocheted around the ward. They all snored at night so I didn't sleep much. I was in a bed near the window and I could look down the drive of Dr Grays, and see who was coming to visit. I was horrified when the nurse told me I had to be shaved, as there was little to shave as I was only 12. The next morning, the nurse asked me if my bowels had moved. I hadn't a clue what she was talking about. When Mum and Fiona came to visit, I told them I fancied a cheese and tomato sandwich. Mum promised she would bring me one the next day. I watched Mum come up the drive at visiting time the next day. I was salivating in anticipation of the sandwich. What a disappointment. The tomatoes, which I like hard, were soft and the sandwich was soggy. I went home and had to take it easy for a few days before I went back to have my stitches out. I was expecting the nurse to rip the plaster off but she was very gentle. I could see the wound for the first time. There were thick black stitches which looked like they had been done using buttonhole twist and broad silver clamps like broad staples with teeth. I was rigid with fear as each one was removed. The clips were easy, but the stitches pulled as the nurse snipped them open and tweezed them out and I was glad when it was all over with. Soon the itching healing began and it didn't take me long to recover, go back to school and play again.

Mum tried to build me up. Most breakfasts we had what Mum called morning rolls. It took me 50 years to track them down and they are not called morning rolls at all. They are butteries, a regional delicacy from Aberdeenshire. I remember them tasting like croissants, but salty and that's exactly right. We were on holiday in Wick and spotted them in a small bakery window. Butteries, or rowies, were originally made for the sailors and the extra salt was a preservative. The Hairy Bikers made them on their trip to Aberdeen and the recipe is in one of their books. You can buy butteries in Morrisons in Inverness. We had to suck and eat marrow out of bones when Mum made soup, and have a daily spoon of malt extract and cod liver oil, all of which are supposed to be very good for you.

Mum used her extra money to start redecorating the house. She was extremely house proud and I have even seen her on the floor with a magnifying glass making sure it was clean. Sometimes, she got us to dust and she always checked when we had finished so you had to make sure you had dusted everything including underneath the table. Our bedroom was painted and we got new parchment lampshades which clipped on to the headboard and we had our own switch on each bed. We got candlewick bedspreads and sat our teddies and dolls neatly on them.
In Germany, Mum had been reminded of the qualities of continental quilts, which is what they were first called. Here everybody had blankets. Mum collected feather pillows from wherever she could which was usually the jumble sales. The feathers were washed in small quantities, put in a pillowcase, and hung out to dry on the washing line. Sometimes there were six of them blowing in the wind. She bought some feather ticking which was a very closely woven cotton fabric to stop the feathers poking out. She made two huge cases which were to be the quilts. The feathers were inserted and we did a lot of sneezing before the ends were sewn up. In Germany pillows are big and square so she made some of those for us as well. We were the first for many a mile to have them. Most people hadn't even heard of them but they did have their drawbacks. All the feather seemed to roll to the top or bottom or side leaving the middle bit cold. She had to remake them putting in channels to stop the feathers moving about so much. It took some getting used to after years of being tucked in with blankets. As often as possible the quilts were hung on the line to air and then vigorously shaken.
Mum didn't have a quilt; maybe my father didn't want one. She bought a beautiful olive green eiderdown with a honeycomb centre. I never knew that eiderdown came from eider ducks and is exclusively collected from their nests. The female plucks the feathers from her breast to use in the nest. It is collected and replaced with straw. Nowadays most of it is farmed in Iceland. That's why it's so expensive.
 I had a nosey in the tall cupboard in Mum's bedroom and found my Christmas present which was a huge Chambers dictionary which I

have used all my life. I also found bath salts and Herbie who was our hibernating tortoise.

When yoyos and hula hoops came in we learned how to play with them, and so did Mum. She loved the hula hoop and was very good at it. There was always someone to play with and always a competitive element to games. Hopscotch was very popular and all you needed was a stone and a piece of chalk. You had to jump up and down the laid our grid and then you could claim your box. Nobody else could use that box and so the game became progressively more difficult. The person with the most boxes won.

Stamp collecting was very popular and a good way to learn geography. You sent for your stamps on approval from Stanley Gibbons in Bridgenorth. You could claim lots of free ones and there were usually imitation penny blacks which you fantasised about as being real and worth a fortune. You took out the ones you wanted to pay for, and sent the others back. You had to decide how to arrange your stamps and attach them with special stamp hinges which meant the stamps cold be easily removed. I liked the ones with flowers, animals and birds best. They were usually from what was then called Magyar Posta and is now Hungary. There were different sections in the catalogue and I enjoyed looking at the ones from The Commonwealth. There was a map in the album so you could find which country the stamps came from. I never thought about the possibility of visiting any of these countries.

We went to Saturday matinees at The Two Red Shoes. Children went in with their shilling, which is the equivalent of five pence now. Half your shilling paid for the entrance and the rest you could spend on sweets or an ice lolly. The usherette was an old and ample lady with her hair plaited and coiled round her ears in coils. We called her the dough ring lady.
The cinema showed lots of Westerns like the Lone Ranger with his mask and silver bullet, his horse Silver and his sidekick Tonto who always said "Kemo Sabi" whatever that means. There were cartoons with Donald Duck and the terrifying Zorro with his sword, black cape and mask. I liked the Eastern European films dubbed over in English. It was the highlight of our week but must have been a

nightmare for the usherette and heaven for the parents who got a few hours peace as they didn't have to stay.

With my sixpence I bought. Lucky Tatties and Lucky Bags. Lucky Tatties were large cinnamon dusted sweets about the size of a child's palm. Inside each tattie was the plastic charm like a Scottie dog, a black cat, a cowboy or a car. Children collected them and swapped any doubles. I kept mine in a McGowan's toffee tin. One of the children whose mother was called Moira, swapped and gave me something very special. Mum told me to take it back as it was valuable but Moira said I could keep it. It was a small rose gold pendant with a picture of a beautiful Indian Princess under a glass dome. The Gordon Highlanders spent more than 60 years in India so perhaps a soldier brought it back. Perhaps it was Moira's ex-husband as she lived without a man. Maybe the princess had not been so lucky for Moira. The lucky bags contained an assortment of sweets like a sherbet fountain, bubble gum, a gob stopper or love hearts.

I kept my Princess pendant in the button box for many years which was appropriate. In Platt Fields Costume Museum in Manchester they have a huge button collection and I found some military type buttons with the same Princess. I believe her to be a consort.

My research says The Two Red Shoes is a ballroom but I only knew it as a cinema. I found out, as an avid fan that The Beatles played there on 3rd January 1963 whilst I was still living there. There were buses laid on to take people to and from Forres, Buckie, Lossiemouth and other places on the coast. I missed my chance to see them but Mum could probably not have afforded the ticket. I bet Biff Cochrane had tickets but we will come to her later. The Shoes, as it was known, became one of the best-known pop venues in Scotland. People who appeared there included Anita Harris, the Baron Knights and Dave Berry who hid behind his upturned collar and mike while he sang my favourite, The Crying Game."

By this time, we had rented a black and white TV and so were starting to be influenced by the advertising. I remember one for hair curlers called Spoolies which were made of rubber. You twisted your hair round the shaft and then pulled the rubber over to secure. The jingle was "For beauty truly, use a Spoolie". Then there was Green Goddess shampoo with a big green jewel floating down the bottle. We had plenty of eggs so, we mixed egg with the shampoo which turned it blue. You did have to wash it out but in the days before conditioner it worked. There was another shampoo called Clinic which was blue. That became green when the egg was added. We watched programmes like Bill and Ben, Rag Tag and Bobtail, and the Woodentops puppets with Spotty Dog which is now regularly referenced in exercise classes. These were more for Fiona's age group but any TV was a novelty. I liked Junior Criss Cross Quiz and Hirum Holiday and Mr. Ed the talking horse who said "Hi, my name is Mr. Ed." Another favourite was The Magic Boomerang. If you had it and threw it, everything under it stood stock still. I imagined robbing a bank before it came back. There was another about a boy with a pair of slippers with turned up toes and a bells on. When he wore them he could run like the wind which would have been handy to get yourself out of trouble. Of course there were magic carpets to ride on.

The most influential programme on TV for children was Blue Peter with Valerie Singleton, John Noakes and Shep the dog. It was an educational programme which of course still runs today. It taught you to make simple curtains and embellish them with potato prints and how to make a table from a tea chest. Every programme had something to make from packaging. It was aimed at pre-teens. There was no daytime TV then and children's programmes started in the early evening with a choice of two channels, BBC and ITV.

On 22nd November 1963 I watched the news announcing the assassination of President Kennedy. It was one of those shock headlines that stop you in your tracks and all your life you remember where you were when it was announced. Mum found the Kennedy family fascinating, elegant, rich, powerful and like film stars which of course they were.

Mum was also influenced by the power of advertising so we went to Woollies where she bought some Ponds Vanishing Cream which was made to make blemishes vanish. Mum always hated her Roman nose so she got a ruler and eyebrow pencil and drew a line down the bridge of her nose the size she wanted it to be and, applied Vanishing Cream. She thought she would wake up in the morning with a button nose. Obviously not.

On another occasion she bought some Rimmel hair dye in a brown glass bottle. The liquid inside the bottle was purple. Maybe she didn't read the instructions properly as her hair turned the colour of the liquid – purple. I have never seen her in such a state. A hairdresser was an expensive luxury then so Mum got the abrasive powdered scourer called Vim and tried to scrub it out. It didn't matter how much vim and vigour she put into it, it wouldn't budge. So she got the bleach on and finally had to go to the hairdresser. She came back with short hair but it was better than the colour purple!

I loved the adaptation of The Silver Sword by Ian Serrailler. It is a story about a man who escaped from a Nazi prison and goes back to Warsaw to find his wife and children. When he gets there, his home and the area around it is nothing but a pile of rubble and his wife has been taken by the Nazis. He meets a clever orphan boy called Jan who helps him. The silver sword talisman is in fact a paper knife and it accompanies them on their dangerous journey. In one clip a man goes up to a child and magic's an egg from behind his ear. Food of any kind was very scarce so this was miraculous. I went to bed after every episode dreaming about swords coming out of the wall so I pulled the covers over my head.

Mum brought her Honer mouth organ back from Germany and we were mesmerised when she played. She made us listen to Larry Adler and she mimicked him playing. Adler must have been good as he later collaborated with Sting, Elton John, Kate Bush and Cerys Matthews. The radio was always on and Mum sang along with every genre of music.

The ice cream man often came playing his jingly tune. We sometimes had ice cream and the man always asked us if we wanted monkey's blood on it. That's far more fun than raspberry juice. I still find it hard to believe that Buggerlugs would buy himself sweets and not give us any. He would keep them down the side of his chair and just eat them all without ever offering us any. Maybe Mum's money had become a bone of contention but I don't know how any father can do that.
One night, you could have cut the air with a knife. Fiona and I were on the rug with our pyjamas on watching TV. We were resting our

heads in our hands and lying on our tummies with our legs bent at the knee. He decided to start an argument and told Mum we would never amount to anything. The best we could do was go and work in Woollies and he said we were whores. This was said in front of us and we knew it was time to make ourselves scarce. Comments like this were just more nails in the coffin.

We were unaware of the changes science was making to the ordinary things we bought. The TV replaced the fire as the focal point in our houses. Petrochemicals gave us paint of every colour and pattern. We had pale grey wallpaper with cabbage roses in white and black. We also had feature walls with the same wallpaper in black with grey and white roses. Feature walls are again making a revival. Almost everything comes full circle in one way or another. It was the same in the bathroom. We had black wallpaper with coloured tropical angelfish. On the opposite wall it was white paper with the same coloured fish. There was even gold and silver on the paper. This was all a far cry from the drab narrow range of colours up until now.

When He was in the bath and we needed to go to the loo, we had to knock on the door and wait before we entered. This gave him time to put a flannel on his privates. I did like to watch him shaving with his badger hair shaving brush and solid shaving soap which he lathered all over. His silver Gillette razor often needed new blades and I watched him put them in and then put on his Old Spice aftershave. He combed his hair and put Brylcreem on. It had a distinctive smell and made hair look shiny so it could be styled. Although it sounds American it was made in Birmingham and was the forerunner of all modern hair grooming products for men. It is still on sale today in different packaging.

Buggerlugs had a very annoying habit of jingling the coins in his pockets. Men did not have purses and instead wore holes in their pockets with the very heavy coins. Just one penny then was four times the size of one now. He walked around whistling everywhere which most men did. It becomes irritating when it's the same tune over and over again and it certainly got on Mum's nerves. She told him off for jingling the money in his "bleddy pooches".

We had some new worktops put in the tiny kitchen. We had a boiler for the washing with an agitator and a swing over mangle. I remember the wonderful smell of Evo Stick on the new Formica tops. The worktops were yellow and Mum managed to get some plastic accessories. She bought yellow polka-dot egg cups, toast rack and salt and pepper pots. These were the very latest thing to have as plastic was a relatively new material.

Mum worked hard and was probably tired the day she put salt in the washing machine and Daz in the potatoes. It was just like the story of the Magic Porridge Pot as the bubbles spilled out of the pot, down the cooker and ran along the floor. We gave her the name "Burner and Shrinker" after that.

There was also room for a very small table and chairs and this is where we had our meals. Buggerlugs would hit us with the knife across the knuckles if we did or said anything wrong.

Our puddings were tinned peaches, pears or fruit cocktail and always with Carnation condensed milk. Sometimes the milk was whisked with sugar to make it thicker. It was very good. There was instant whip which when mixed with milk made a lovely mousse-type desert. The main course would be something like a couple of slices of boiled ham with a tomato and some chipples which were like matchstick chips. Mum was good at making chips and always from scratch and as she never left the pan unattended she managed not to set the kitchen on fire. Chips were fried in lard and we always had them with salad cream or mayonnaise, which is the continental way. Her culinary skills improved a little and she developed some more exotic recipes. We often had rolled up lettuce leaves with sugar inside. It was anything to make us eat our greens. The best was toast, which was liberally spread with butter then heaped with sugar and returned to the grill to caramelise. Minutes later, bubbling hot and nicely browned it came out to cool. It was a bit like having toffee on buttered toast.

The kitchen was also the gambling den and while we were in bed He brought his friends in to play cards and drink whisky. Our room was above so we could hear every word. In the morning the smell of stale Senior Service and alcohol clung in the air. Mum found it difficult to get rid of the smell.

When she was nine Fiona got chicken pox and after the incubation period, so did I. We were covered in pink calamine lotion with the instruction not to pick the spots which of course we both did and have several pock marks and we had to stay in bed. To add insult to injury, I started my periods. I knew all about them as Mum wasn't going to do what her mother did and leave it to somebody else. We were well up on the facts of life. By this time, I was 13 and had left primary school and was a pupil at Elgin Academy. The boys were always trying to find out who was "on" by smacking us on the bottom to see if we were wearing a towel. It was a badge of honour to have started.

Mum bought a new radio and hairdryer which clipped on to the back of a chair. There was a flexible hose which attached to the hairdryer and this blew warm air into the hood. Mum sat underneath in her curlers like the Queen. Sometimes she had a perm with small blue and pink curlers. You did something with a perming solution, wrapper a paper round your hair and put the curler in. The solution was pungent and eye watering.

Mum didn't have many things for herself, so she must have been distressed when Fiona and I were chasing each other round the settee and the chair one day, and her precious hairdryer fell on to the floor and smashed into several pieces. But she never told us off. She went and got some UHU glue and managed to stick all the pieces together and it was still working. Another time Fiona and I were fighting and she threw the scissors at me. I ducked and they went through the new radio. It must have been upsetting for her to see her prized possessions being broken and I feel guilty just thinking about it.

I probably became a little rebellious and on one occasion Mum hit me on the backside with the carpet beater and I had pattern marks to prove it. I remember being chased upstairs and lying on the landing pretending to be dead. Eventually it stopped. Thank God now we have carpets which don't need beating. I still cringe when I see them in antique shops. Fiona bought me one as a joke. I have a one twelfth scale dolls house which my son Danny made for me when he was 16 and I have a miniature carpet beater in there.

As I mentioned before, Mum was deeply spiritual. Maybe she was thinking spare the rod and spoil the child as she was hitting me. When I was little she was told by a fortune teller that I was born with a silver spoon in my mouth. If I was it is a salt spoon. I used to think it meant you were lucky but the literal meaning is that someone familial gives you a foot up the ladder. Well there was nothing like that. She believed particularly in an American Christian Evangelist Baptist Minister called Billy Graham and always watched his broadcasts on TV. All this makes her sound loopy but these were very common beliefs at the time.

We had a grey and white cat called Sparkie named after the talking piano. Sparkie used to sit on top of the gate post and didn't seem to be bothered by the red ants. He was waiting for Him to come home. At least there was one thing he loved. When the baker's van came, Sparkie went in the van and always came out with a scotch pancake. He dragged it between his legs to somewhere safe so he could eat it. He was a local celebrity and everybody knew he did this.

All the books we had from school had to be backed with brown paper. This was my father's job and something he was very good at. The books were covered with the accuracy of a draftsman and he wrote our name on, the subject and the class we were in. He always wrote with capital letters as many people did then. It is a sign of a limited education that people could not join the script. Mum on the other hand always write in an odd joined script on squared paper as they did in Germany. He also sharpened our pencils to a point with a knife almost as if he were going to whittle it into something else. As soon as we could we covered the books in graffiti.

Chapter 11. The Folks frae Elgin

Next door to us lived a woman and her teenage son who mostly kept themselves to themselves. There was a piano up against the party wall as the boy was learning to play and it drove Mum berserk. He could only play one tune over and over again. It was a tune called "In an English Country Garden". I can hear Mum now complaining about him playing that "bleddy" tune in her German accent.

Next door to her lived Mrs. Nicholson. She was always out on the street telling us to shut up. She had no children of her own and wasn't used to the noise. We got a silent revenge when we saw a chocolate brown pair of bloomers on the washing line like Mum had, so from then on Mrs. Nicholson got the nickname Chocolate Drawers. Very childish, I know. but we were children.
We enjoyed silly limericks like –
"*Milk, milk, lemonade, round the corner chocolate made*", which referred to our bodily functions.
Or,
Captain Cook was making soup and his wife was making jelly.
Captain cook fell into the soup and burned his rubber belly.

Another favourite was:
Auntie Mary had a canary up the leg of her drawers,
when she farted down it darted, down the leg of her drawers.
As the saying goes, small things amuse small minds.

Two doors down from Chocolate Drawers lived the Reid family. There was Billy, who was older than us, and he rode a huge Norton motor bike. Then there was Elma or Elizabeth Mary, who was round about our age and was a good friend who we played with a lot.

Further round the road lived the Toy family, who came from London. They were an army family and I was aware of lots of service personnel in the area. I was allowed once to go upstairs with Linda Toy to see her brother's monkey. The whole of the back bedroom was a cage for this animal. Her brother probably brought it back after one of his tours of duty as it was common then for people to keep exotic animals as pets.

A bit further round the corner there was a man who kept a huge owl in his living room and he fed it day-old chicks.

Opposite our house lived the Walker family. Brenda was a friend we often played with. Her grandmother lived in the same house and she had long grey hair done up in a bun. Once a year on a very hot day she would wash her hair and then she would sit outside and let the sun dry her now white hair. She was adamant washing your hair stripped it of its natural oils. In all the time we lived in Scotland I don't ever remember anyone having nits. That was reserved for Fiona later.

Mrs. Laing was a tall masculine looking woman with budgie eyes, but she was very friendly and invited us in and gave us biscuits. She also had a blue budgie called Jockey who had the same eyes as her.

Further down the road lived the Younies. Mrs Younie was a statuesque woman and her husband was tiny. They had two children: Norma, who was a bit older than us and her brother Iain, who was lovely and sat next to me at school in our double desk. He set up a Beatles club in his bedroom. We played Beatles music on a record player and Iain was always Ringo on the drum kit or biscuit tin. We played air guitars and sang the lyrics.

We all played together, games which included a mocked up tossing the caber which was a short fat pole and a sport at the Highland Games. The best game, though, was group skipping with a long rope and the lovely skipping rhymes such as:
Salt, mustard, vinegar, pepper said over and over getting faster and faster till you were sure to trip. Whoever was out had to take the end of the rope so everybody had a chance.
Other rhymes were:
"*Up in the north a long way off a donkey caught the whooping cough,*
What shall we give him to make him better? Salt, mustard, vinegar,

pepper."

*"Granny's in the kitchen doing a bit of stitching,
In comes a bogey man and chases Granny out."*

Marbles or "doolies" were also popular. You could get a big bag of marbles from Woollies and it was great looking into each one and seeing the colours, wondering how they got in there. Mum made us both a drawstring bag to put them in. It was a lovely feeling winning them, but not losing them or when they broke. Our games very rarely interrupted by cars as these were few and far between.

It was late October in our last year at primary school and everyone was collecting wood and rubbish for the annual bonfire. In the middle of Muirfied Road was a communal green and that's where it was, piled high with chairs and sofas and a guy on the top. Almost every child made a guy and went round asking for "a penny for the guy please." November 5th came and everybody was excited to go home from school. When we had had our tea we all trooped over to see what now would be regarded as pathetic fireworks and to watch the bonfire and the burning of the guy. It was to be the last time I would be close to fireworks or a bonfire for decades.
The next day, the seat next to me was empty. Iain had gone to the cubs' bonfire and he had returned to a firework which did not go off. It blew up in his face, killing him. The school closed on the day of his funeral and I can remember the hearse arriving at his house to collect his parents. This incident has had a knock on effect for the whole of my life. After that, we watched the bonfire and fireworks from the bedroom window. My daughter Grace was born on of November 6th. I went into labour on the night of the 5th and I am sure the fact that my husband went back to an unlit firework started me off in labour.

I was in the Brownies for a short time, but the minute it was suggested that cubs and brownies go to camp together that was it. I was removed from the Brownies by Mum. She was also worried about the forkies if we went camping. Forkies, or earwigs, had forky tails and the belief was that they crawled inside your ear and burst your eardrum.

Most children would have had access to "A Child's Garden of Verse" by Robert Louis Stephenson. He really understood the way children thought. Otherwise, how could he have written a poem like:
*"In winter I get up at night and dress by golden candle light.
In summer when I want to play I have to go to bed by day."*

One day I saw Prince Charles in his pale grey Gordonstoun School uniform. He was riding his bike and probably trying to get away from the school he called "a prison sentence; Colditz with kilts". The school was famous for its Spartan regime. Prince Philip, Princess Anne and Princes Andrew and Edward went there and thrived. Prince Charles did not. He vowed not to send his children there and of course he didn't.

I still find it hard to believe that Onion Johnnies came to Muirfield Road, but they did. They were Breton farmers and labourers on bicycles, who sold pink onions door to door all over Great Britain. They were a long way from home, dressed in striped shirts and wearing a beret. The fashion world now calls this the Breton tee shirt. The onions, garlic and shallots hung over the handlebars of their bikes and over their shoulders. This is the stereotypical image of a Frenchman. The Onion Johnnie came from the area around Roscoff in Brittany and they found the market more profitable here. They brought their harvest across the channel in July and stored them in rented barns. By the 50s the numbers were dwindling so we were lucky to see one every year we lived there. There were still 160 of them trading in 1973 and they were the inspiration for farmers to set up Britanny Ferries in 1970. There is an Onion Johnnie Museum in Roscoff which opened in 2004 and every year there is an onion festival. I have promised myself that one day I will go and see the museum and the festival.

Sometimes I went to the baths with Elma. On the way back we would get chips and a huge pickled onion. Along with the chips we had mealy Jimmies which were deep fried sausages made of oatmeal. They were very claggy when you ate them but delicious.

I loved school and went to Elgin Academy from 1962-4, from the ages 12-14. I was becoming a teenager which was new terminology.

I particularly enjoyed English Grammar. We learned about a malapropism which was of great interest to me. Mrs. Malaprop was a character in a Sheridan play called "The Rivals." Suddenly I had an "Isaac Newton" moment as my Mummy was forever uttering malapropisms. She would often replace an incorrect word for one with a similar sound. One of the best was Shitmans Paste instead of Shippams. Then there was hippix for hiccups and post lorder for postal order and many more.

Apart from the malapropisms, Mum's vocabulary was quite incredible and she picked up lots of folklore sayings that are becoming lost today, such as one drop of vinegar kills ten drops of blood, or a tear for every pearl.

There was another girl at school called Patricia Young so, when I came second in the art exam, I convinced myself there had been a mistake and it was her prize. To this day I'm not sure as I am artistic but not good at painting. There was a boy I fancied called Ainsley Haldane. He went off to live in New Zealand with his family to become sheep farmers which was something I couldn't imagine. We had learned about "the land of the long white cloud" but I couldn't fathom the distance.

In an effort to be a better cook than Mum I listened carefully during domestic science lessons. I made apple pie in an oval white enamel pie dish. I made shortcrust pastry, stewed the apples with sugar and carefully put the lid on the pie with water to stick it. The top had an egg wash and a hole for the steam to escape. It was surprisingly good. The following week and using the same pie dish I made shepherd's pie with lamb and the next week it was mince with a potato topping again in the same dish and finally cottage pie. They were all edible or at least what was left of them by the time I reached home as they all leaked on the long walk home. I made vegetable soup and mutton casserole and these were carried home in a killer jar which was better. We baked scones and pancakes. At the end of the term we had a tea party when the emphasis was on setting the table and proper etiquette. It was the kind of thing you would see in Woman's Weekly. We were being prepared for our roles as wives. Embroidering tray cloths, making tea cosies and aprons.

Biff Cochrane, who I mentioned before, was in the same class. The school was streamed and we were in "1a2," "1a1" being the elite. Her father owned one of the biggest shops in Elgin, Cochrane's Music shop. Teenagers were just beginning to buy records by The Beatles, Rolling Stones, Manfredd Mann and the Dave Clark 5. Biff, or Elizabeth's father, was Bill Barr Cochrane. He was a war veteran who was born in Elgin. He was an accomplished pianist and violin player, and I didn't know he had a large recording studio in the back of the shop and artists recorded their first discs there.

He was also a box office agent selling tickets for the likes of The Beatles, Billy Smarts and Bertram Mills Circus so I bet Biff got lots of tickets.

Bill was particularly interested in Andy Stewart and gave him a helping hand up the ladder. Andy was an influential singer and entertainer who compered a very popular TV Programme called the White Heather Club. It was a weekly patriotic club, but every year it also hosted Hogmanay. Buggerlugs looked very much like Andy Stewart. Andy had several international hits, including "Donald Where's Yer Troosers?" "Campbelton Loch," and my favourite, "Scottish Soldier". He was a major presence in my life, regularly on TV or singing on the radio.

Bertram Mills circus came to Edinburgh in 1959 and Auntie Molly and Uncle Gus took us. There were lions, tigers and elephants and a pipe band and a massive terrifying stilt walker so I hid behind Uncle Gus. I did love the Big Top, the wonderful ringmaster in his red jacket and top hat and the clowns were marvellous.

One Friday night, a flatbed wagon came on to our road. There was a man on the back tied to a pole and he was jet black and covered in feathers. Another man on the wagon was throwing coins to the children which we eagerly picked up. We learned that the man was going to be married and this was the tradition of tarring and feathering. I remember wondering how he was going to get clean and I have read since that this was never done the night before a wedding so I am consoled that he had time to clean himself.

Another regular visitor to Muirfield Road was the knife sharpener. He came on his bike and he had a big grinding wheel rigged up to the back of the bike. He lifted the bike on to a stand and the grinding wheel turned when he pedalled. He sharpened knives and shears. We must have been doing poetry at school because I remember thinking he was a pedlar.

"I wish I lived in a caravan
With a horse to ride like a pedlar man."
Robert Louis Stephenson

Now I ask myself, where has this love of poetry come from? Could it be that I have inherited something from my father?

Mum was neurotic about making sure we went to the dentist. Aluminum fillings containing mercury were very common at the time. We sometimes trust professional people far too much and believe they are infallible. He must have practised on us as I have several of these and they have only just been phased out.

Mum loved the poet Pam Ayres, this poem of hers:

Oh, I wish I'd looked after me teeth,
And spotted the dangers beneath
All the toffees I chewed
And the sweet sticky food.
Oh, I wish I'd looked after me teeth.

One day a card came through the door which looked interesting and the reply was prepaid. I fancied it and thought, why not? Not long afterwards a man came knocking at the door asking for me. I had applied for a savings clock and Mum went bonkers. You had to put the money in to keep the clock going and when the man came to empty the clock he deducted the rent. Mum wasn't having any of it so the clock went back.

I had a big row with Mum about the clock and I decided to leave home. I packed a little bag and told her I was leaving. She asked me where I was going and I told her I was going to Auntie "whatever her name was" who lived in Bishopmill, which was the same place as the dentist was. She stopped me on the drive and I was expecting an outpouring of love and instead she gave me a threepenny bit for the bus fare. Needless to say I went back inside the house with my tail between my legs but I felt deeply wounded and didn't do it again.

I had become a stroppy teenager and I remember wanting a bra. They were called Junior Bras and made by a company called Berleigh. It was made of cotton poplin and had a soft inner bra which allowed room for improvement. Basically it looked like a bandage with holes cut in the inner fabric. My father said I did not need one as I only had fried eggs. I felt deflated before I had the chance to be inflated.

I had been wearing a warm liberty bodice, which was the replacement for the corset. It had rubber buttons and suspenders at the bottom. By the age of 12 this was the last thing you wanted to wear. I did pinch a pair of Mums stockings and as I couldn't find the suspenders, I ruined the precious stocking by using safety pins to attach them.

There was a shop in Elgin near Woollies which was the first shop in Elgin to have an escalator and I fell up it in my white kitten heels. I may have been distracted by the half size busts all the way up on the side which were dressed in the most exquisite bras. I was imagining which ones I could wear very soon. That shop also had those air chutes for notes and money. They use a vacuum to propel cylinders to a central area and are still widely used. I bought my first dress here with the money I made from tattie picking. It was red wool with three quarter length sleeves, a full skirt and a lace jabot and black velvet bow. I loved it, wore it often and kept it for ages.

On the streets of Elgin I never saw anybody disabled as people were institutionalised. Nobody thought about integration of any kind. If you were not "normal" and able-bodied then that's what happened.

Once I saw a black baby and it was gorgeous and fascinating. In the 1950s the government recruited people from the West Indies to work here as there was a huge skills shortfall after the war and also it was part of our responsibility to Commonwealth countries. Mum also knew a black nurse I presume she worked with. It is nothing new that we recruit nurses from overseas. The nurse has two well developed daughters with the whitest clothes I have ever seen in my life. I just thought the mother must have been using OMO which was a washing powder supposed to "add brightness". It never occurred to me it was the contrast of their skin. I was also really jealous of the size of their boobs in comparison to my fried eggs. We are now very much aware of politically correct language but not then. Black people were coloured people then and it was not meant as an insult.

I was beginning to grow up and be more interested in the opposite sex and Fiona became my bodyguard. All the teenagers congregated near the garages. Some things were permissible but others not so a snog was fine but any wandering palms or southern migration and I would call Fiona who was hiding between the garages. She had orders to knee the boys in the balls. On one occasion Mrs Walker came to complain that Fiona had kicked Kenny in the "robin," which was one of many euphemisms for penis which was a taboo word. Eventually the boys kept a look out for my bodyguard.

The man from Encyclopaedia Britannica came with his briefcase and you could buy a volume at a time paying so much per week and there were 32 volumes in total. If you bought them all you got a free bookcase. Needless to say we didn't get any as they were ridiculously expensive. It is no longer printed but published on line where it can be updated. Now we have the wonderful Wikipedia, the online encyclopaedia, without which my research would have been much harder. We did get magazines like Knowledge which was weekly, informative and age appropriate. It was also good as you could cut out pictures and articles to use for school projects.

The filthy coalman came every week and he carried the hessian sacks weighing a hundredweight to wherever you wanted them. We had them in the concrete shed at the bottom of the garden. You gave him a wide berth in case come of the coal dust rubbed off on you. In the shed we kept our pet mice which had been in the house to start off with but Mum said they were too smelly so thy ended up in the shed where they seemed to breed very happily but they always ate their babies.

The Barrs mineral wagon came with crate upon crate of lemonade. I liked the Irn Bru which advertises itself as "made in Scotland from girders." The next time the mineral man came you gave him back the empty bottles and got a few pennies for them. The bottles were the kind that had stoppers attached so you couldn't lose them.

The Mormon Missionaries came from Salt Lake City in Utah to convert the world to the teachings of The Church of Jesus Christ of Latter day saints. Two extremely well dressed fragrant men with hypnotic accents spent many hours at our house, as we did at theirs. Their church was a rented function room at The Station Hotel in Elgin. We were enthralled and completely under their spell. We really enjoyed their teaching, read avidly, said and wrote prayers and became so besotted with these men and this religion that Mum agreed for us to be baptised into the Mormon faith. The preachers were called Elders and the one I had the hots for was Elder Leishman. All the young men have to serve their time as missionaries and they spread the word all over the world. They have left their mark as there are plenty of Churches of Latter Day Saints. Off we went along with many other new recruits on a coach to Aberdeen to be baptised. We put on white gowns and walked into the baptismal pool where we were totally submerged in the water. It was a very strange sight and feeling to see all these people with white ghostly gowns following each other into the water like lemmings.
Buggerlugs didn't go as he thought it was rubbish. The Mormons abstain from alcohol, tobacco, coffee, tea and all stimulants. I remember Mum drinking decaffeinated coffee and tea. She wasn't drinking at this time but the fags she couldn't give up. Mormons give 10% of their income to the church, which is how they pay for the new churches. Our missionaries had done their job and after a few pleasant months they went back to Utah leaving a big hole in our lives and Mum was very unsettled.

At weekends we could hear the skirl of the pipes and it was wonderful. On a Sunday, the Elgin Pipe Band congregated on Muirfield Road as several members of the band lived there. The pipe band leader, resplendent in his uniform headed up the band. He held his mace, and conducted. He wore a huge hat which looks like a busby but is made of feathers. The drum major had a leopard skin across his chest. One of the members of the Gordon regiment donated their kill to the pipe band for ceremonial use. Nowadays this is politically incorrect and fake fur is used. I liked listening to the bagpipes being filled with air and then pressed under the piper's arm as he played the chanter. My favourite was Scotland the Brave. Even now the pipes thrill me and make the hairs on my arms stand on end. The whole ensemble looks and sounds very powerful. All members of the band at this time were serving soldiers. The British Army still has its own pipes and drums facility known as the Army School of Bagpipe Music and Highland Drumming. To be a qualified Pipe Major, candidates must pass a series of courses at the school.

Years later we took Grace and Danny on holiday to Edinburgh and stayed at Kilconquhar Castle. Grace was maybe 5 and Danny 12. There were a couple of pipers on the Golden mile and Grace piped up, "look Mummy hosepipes in quilts!" The day before the children had been arguing about which was correct – a Yak or a Highland cow. That's what happens when you give your child a picture book with Y for Yak! Now they are always referred to as Yaks.

Back in time and out of the blue, Mum started selling all the things which she had spent the last few years buying. We were sworn to secrecy but we knew we were on the move again. Mum had a masterplan and like lambs we would follow.

Chapter 12 Haste ye back.

Farewell then, my Bonnie Scotland. Just one more Scottish step before I become a Sassenach. Farewell to the beautiful places with lyrical names like: Achtermuchtie, Tomintoul, Clackmanus, Fochabers, Drumnadrochit, Craigellachie, Archieston, Cardu, Knockando and Maggieknockater to name a few. Deliciously tongue twisting and Mum could say them all which is more than the Sassenachs could. They couldn't say the ch sound and made ck instead so loch became lock!

Farewell to the football teams, and whilst I have never been interested in football I was always forced to listen to the results and did like listening to East Fife 5- Forfar 4 and the other quintessentially Scottish names especially those with the national flower – the thistle- in.

Farewell to the language I understand well but is alien to southerners. Just a few examples to keep you guessing; a hae tae gang; nae problem; adinna ken; a feel no weel; I'll ge ye a skelpt lug; haud yer wheest; ah am nae dunderheaded eejit; ge us a wee peek; peely wally; sleekit. If ye dinnae stop yer greetin I'll ge ye something tae greet aboot, I'll say cheerio the noo!

We were on the train to Alford.
The sound of the train on the tracks always makes me think of the poem
From a Railway Carriage.

Faster than fairies, faster than witches,
Bridges and houses hedges and ditches,
And charging along like troops in a battle,
All through the meadows the horses and cattle.

Alford is less than two hours away from Elgin and the first stop on Mum's plan. It is a small town in Aberdeenshire just south of the River Don, and the home of Aberdeen Angus cattle. There is a life-size model of a bull on the edge of the town. They are huge black beasts and not to be confused with "yaks." Alford is also famous for its pinhead oatmeal which Mum fried her fish in and which mealy Jimmies are made from.

This is a largely rural farming area and that's exactly where we were going. This really felt like a holiday and on a farm. We met Mr. Grant and his two strapping sons and his lovely daughter Mary. We always knew how to behave and Mum only had to give us "the look" to make us freeze. I think this was an informal interview with Mr. Grant who was a Polish immigrant and he too had an accent. He had two Alsatians. Fiona and I found it impossible to contain ourselves when he announced, "The docks are very wise you know." In our world, your dock was your bottom. We collapsed in fits of the giggles. The dogs had wise bottoms.

Would you believe even these dogs had their names changed? They were called German Shepherd's but in the run up to WW2 it was thought even having a name with German in it, would hinder the popularity of the dog so it was changed to Alsatian, after the French-German border city of Alsace. In 1925 it was changed back to German Shepherd. How fickle we are.

When eventually we composed ourselves about the dogs with wise bottoms, we were allowed to play the piano in the other room. We were here only a few weeks but it was brilliant. The house had a huge kitchen with a range cooker. The bedrooms were off a long corridor and our room was at the end with Mary's opposite. She was a few years older than I was but obviously craved female company. She helped me to use her make-up and gave me a lipstick. She had black wavy hair and looked striking when she wore her red lipstick. We didn't see much of the men as they were out working. There was a barn full of bales of hay and Fiona and I loved playing in there. We climbed the bales and made dens and it was magic. In the front of the barn there were pigs in a sty. Fiona and I were shocked to see the pig mount the sow. The pig had a huge long penis like a corkscrew! For the rest of the time we were there we watched the pigs with great interest. Even Mum came to have a look. Apparently, that's where the saying "Let me screw you" comes from.

One night we went with the Grants in their lorry to the cinema.

When we came back the sons had to start up the generator as the farm was not on mains electricity. It took forever before we had power. I don't know if this was a deciding factor or not, but Mum decided not to stay.
We were on another train.

All of the sights of the hill and the plain
Fly as thick as driving rain:
And ever again, in the wink of an eye,
Painted stations whistle by.

Blackwall. London.
Blackwall is in the East end of London in the borough of Tower Hamlets on the north bank of the River Thames and on the corner of the peninsula of the Isle of Dogs.
The single gentleman Mum came to see here was Mr. Black. The house was terraced and in front was the Docklands light railway. It all seemed very grimy but like sheep we followed and never complained. Behind the front door was a long dark corridor leading to the kitchen at the back of the house. The house was weird and we can't have stayed here for more than a couple of nights. The bedroom we slept in was at the front of the house and it was noisy, not only from the traffic but the trains. In the bedroom there were several cages with birds in on a table at the end of the bed. We slept very little and Mum saw a ghost. She was describing it to us and asking us if we could see it which we couldn't. In the morning when she told Mr Black, he said the ghost was his wife who had died. That was it and off we went again. I didn't have the word to describe it then but I do now – surreal. I'm not surprised Mum scarpered.

Here is a child who clambers and scrambles,
All by himself and gathering brambles;
Here is a tramp who stands and gazes,
And there is the green for stringing daisies!

Sevenoaks, Kent.
Sevenoaks is 21 miles south east of Charing Cross on a main commuter line. We were in an area called Swanley. It was fairly straightforward for Mum to get here. The house was a bungalow and

we had never been in one before. There was a lady in the house and I have no idea what was wrong with her but she never spoke to us. The man of the house we called Uncle Ron. He was a lovely moustachioed man who looked like an ex-serviceman. I have very happy memories of sitting round the breakfast table in the kitchen. Mum and Ron listened to the radio and sang. They were obviously getting on like a house on fire. Ron was very thoughtful; he took us shopping into London in his car. We went to British Home Stores and we had never seen a department store before. The variety and choice was amazing. I got a new pair of orange frilly tennis knickers. I think maybe Ron could see I was growing up and needed the company of other teenagers. He took me to the local youth club and collected me later. There was a ping pong table and lots of music. The song I remember most was The Beatles "You can't do that." Mum had her own bedroom and I watched her put cream on her face. It was in a plastic bottle with a gold top and it was called Revlon Moondrops and she let me use some. Her perfume was called Apple Blossom by Helena Rubenstein. Ron had bought both the cream and the perfume for her.

There was still not much sign of Ron's wife. The only thing I noticed and was disgusted by was that she put her used sanitary towels wrapped in newspaper in the toilet bin for Mum to clean.

Brands Hatch is also in Swanley and we could see and hear it from the back garden. Ron took us there and we watched the practise runs. The noise was earthy and incredible and we were enjoying ourselves and loving every minute. It must have been school holidays as it was never mentioned. I went to the youth centre a few times and was beginning to feel settled.

I should have known something would go wrong. Mum fell hook, line and sinker for Ron and the feeling was mutual. Mum said she couldn't do that to his wife, so she made the next appointment in London and this one I remember well and was not impressed. Ron knew what she was doing so it made it easy. Soon we were off again and we were very sorry to go. This would have been a good place to stay and or lives would have been very different.

Here is a cart run away in the road
Lumping along with man and load;
And here is a mill and there is a river:

Each a glimpse and gone forever!

Robert Louis Stevenson

Chapter 13 Moss Lane East Rusholme Manchester.

1964-1970

*"Dirty British Coaster with a salt-caked smoke stack,
Butting through the Channel in the mad march days,
With a cargo of Tyne coal,
Road-rails, pig lead,
Firewood, iron-ware, and cheap tin trays"
Abridged
John Masefield.*
This verse of the poem seems to sum up Cottonopolis and the Manchester Ship Canal. The huge chimneys belching out smoke and leaving the air heavily polluted with smog and giving the city the very unhealthy title of Chimney of the World.

We arrived at Manchester's Central Station, which was dilapidated, filthy and with many broken windows. Once the single span roof would have been beautiful but by the time we arrived, it was near to the end of its days. It's a grade 11 listed building, now known as Manchester Central, and is used among other things for party political conferences.

With our cardboard suitcases we then had to get the number 44 bus to Whitworth Park. We walked through the park with our mouths open is disbelief. We had never seen such dirty black buildings. We sat on the stone steps outside 434. We rang the door bell but Eric was late and we had to wait for him. Mum was already talking about moving on. We were now known as children from a broken home and we certainly felt something was broken.

Eric arrived in his van and apologised but this was not a promising start. He opened the door to a long corridor. On the left hand side was a Victorian hall stand in keeping with the house and an alabaster dog which would become a weapon to protect us when we answered the door. On the right, the front room of the house was piled high with furniture and bric-a-brac. I remember taxidermy birds in a glass dome and cuckoo clock. Next to that there was another sparsely furnished room. Further down the corridor and down a step, was the room and the kitchen where Eric lived.

He welcomed us with a smile. This man was no oil painting. We met him in London very briefly when we were in Sevenoaks. He was divorced and was desperate to have children in his huge house. I guess this was the main attraction for Mum. On the way upstairs he showed us the first room. It was almost empty but even then I was struck by the wallpaper, which was a chinoiserie pattern with a matching border. The next room was the bathroom with beautiful tiles. Then a toilet room with a high flush and a step up. Up another step was Eric's bedroom. Then a room which ran the length of the front of the house. This was also nearly empty. Up the final flight of stairs and through a locked door to our flat. There was a large living room with very high ceilings as all the rooms had. It had a single bed, a sideboard, a table and chairs and a settee.

The single sash window looked down over the garden and Playfair Street. There was a tiny kitchen, and if you stood in the middle you could touch everything. It had one of those 1940s larder cupboards with the drop down front and that was the only worktop there was. Up a few more steps to another bedroom with two single beds, for Fiona and me to sleep in. It even had fitted wardrobes and cupboards. The house was enormous and there was also a cellar which we were told once housed servants. There was an ancient standard lamp with a parchment shade like a daffodil which was discarded there, a remnant of another life.

Once these grand Victorian villas curved around Whitworth Park in a huge cul-de-sac but most were demolished to build Manchester Royal Infirmary so only a few remained. Much later we met a lady from a few doors down and we called her Mrs. Major because she was married to a major. She said she remembered when merchants lived in the houses and rode around in horses and carriages. How sad then to witness this faded grandeur.

Reluctantly we unpacked our cases. Eric went to work every day and left Mum to make a home for him and us. He had a van and a car, and a business on back George Street Manchester, called the Belt, Button and Valet Service. It wasn't long before he took us to his factory and although it looked a mess he knew where everything was. There were piles of belts of different colours all tied up and ready to be delivered and thousands of different kinds of buttons and trimmings. I have never been near anything which is more aptly described as "Aladdin's Cave". He had an answering machine instead of a secretary and in some ways was ahead of his time. He had one worker at the factory called Ada. She was the general dogsbody and kept things ticking over. She was small, with tightly curled white hair and loose false teeth which often dropped when she spoke. There were Victorian cast iron machines screwed to the floor. A couple of these were eyelet machines and the eyelets came from a feed above. You put the hole from the belt under the feed and then using your foot, pressed the eyelet into the belt. You could have put thousands in in a day and it wasn't long before Mum managed to fire an eyelet through her thumb and then there was a trip to hospital. Once it was removed all they could do was dress it but it was a while before she could put any eyelets in again. It went straight through to the bone and was excruciatingly painful.

Industrial sewing machines and cutting machines cut the correct size of fabric and stiffener for self-covered buttons. It was scary and fascinating at the same time. Eric also had outworkers who did piece work and got paid by the item. This was exploitation of women but not seen to be so at the time. They worked for so called "pin money." Once a week Eric collected and paid his outworkers and brought the belts back to the factory for finishing. He delivered the orders himself to his customers and it wasn't long before the factory became a big part of our lives.

Fiona and I finally confessed to Mum about what had been happening to us with my father, Willie's brother and my grandfather. She was shocked and made an appointment for us to see the doctor on Hathersage Road. Now how do you find out if a girl is a virgin or not? Well, you give two young girls an internal to see if the hymen has been broken. Had we not been through enough? The tall respectable-looking doctor, with white hair and another of those with budgie eyes, pronounced that we were both still virgo intacta. We will never forget it. Was it a satisfactory end to an unsavoury experience? No I just felt violated again but you just have to get on with it. It was never spoken about again.

The buildings everywhere were filthy because the factory chimneys spewed out smoke from solid fuel and people also used coal at home. There had been many attempts to clean up the city but it was the Clean Air Act of 1956 that had the swift effect of lifting the smog. Manchester was not alone with its "pea soupers". The last smog was in 1969 and I remember it. The bus conductors often walked in front of bus to guide the driver or buses didn't run at all. It was hard to see your hand in front of face and you could just about make out streetlights, but that was all you had to guide you. We walked in the street with lots of other people who seemed to collect each other along the way. The all-permeating smell of soot clung to your clothes and hair and stayed up your nose, resulting in black snot the next day!

Manchester Town Hall and most of the other buildings have been restored to their former glory but the inner sanctum has been left black and is used for filming period dramas like Frankenstein.
The most important topic of conversation in Manchester is not the national obsession with the weather, but football. With two teams, City and United, there is always banter. It's one of the first questions you are asked. Which team do you support? At first I had no idea as it was not something I was interested in. City's ground was then at Maine Road, about 500yards away from Eric's. On match days you could hear the roar of the crowd and watch the supporters making their way to the ground. The number 53 bus was always full, with mostly men wearing their scarves and turning their deafening football rattles. I decided United were the most popular so I latched on to them so that I could feign an interest, but really it was more to be able to converse with the opposite sex.

Chapter 14 Central Grammar School for Girls.

It was time to sort out schools. Fiona was still of primary school age and she went to the local Heald Place. The nearest secondary school was Ducie High School on Denmark Road which would have been within walking distance. After taking advice Mum decided this was not for me. I wonder how different things would be if I had gone to Ducie, which was a multi-ethnic school even then.
Mum took me to the town hall and we had to wait in a corridor to be seen by some official who gave Mum a cheque. She was told to go to Lewis's or J.M Barrie stores to get my school uniform. As she didn't have a well-paid job Mum was entitled to benefits for us. It would be a long time before supermarkets started selling generic uniforms and the uniform for Central Grammar was comprehensive, expensive and beyond anything I could ever have imagined.

There was a summer and a winter uniform. The winter uniform was a grass green gabardine coat, a blazer with the school crest, a grey pleated skirt and cardigan or jumper, with yellow and green stripes in the cuffs and neck, a custard yellow blouse with a green tie with yellow and red diagonal stripes. I mustn't forget the hat! It was a green velour jockey cap edged in black, and when you took it off it had to be carefully folded down the middle. The summer uniform was a striped dress, either purple, green and white or yellow green and white and the hat was a straw boater. The PE kit was a yellow aertex top and thick grey knickers. There was also a science overall and none of it cost us a penny. This was a time when education was truly egalitarian so children from poor families could get the same education as much better off families, and it gave me a chance to "leapfrog over my competitors." I was extremely lucky and will always be grateful for the politics of the time, both with a large and a small p. Mum believed that education was one of the best ways to achieve social mobility, you can bring a horse to water but you cannot make it drink and Fiona didn't want to drink from the water of education and left school at the earliest opportunity.

I had to get the bus to school – Central Grammar School for Girls on Whitworth Street in the City Centre. What a school this was. I couldn't have gone to a better place if my parents were rich and had sent me to boarding school. The teachers wore gowns and mortar boards and it was extremely formal and fiercely academic.

The Duke of Devonshire opened the magnificent red-bricked, five-storey building in 1900. At the outbreak of the Great War in 1914 the building became a hospital. It was initially a boys' and girls' school but the school was carefully divided so pupils never met. By 1963 the boys had moved to Belle Vue and the space was occupied by Mather College of Education, a teacher training college, where I was heading but could not. Imagine that I would be given such an opportunity or had the brains to do it. The school is no more and it is now apartments and Sheena Simon College. We were warmly welcomed into the old building when we went on a school reunion and it certainly brought back lovely memories.

At the side of the school runs the Rochdale Canal. It is the beginning of the Gay Village and is known locally as Anal Street rather than Canal Street. There is a small park at the front of the school and there is a statue of Alan Turing seated on a bench. He would be happy to have been given a posthumous pardon and a place not only in history but in the Gay Village.

The head of the school was Miss Elizabeth Maude Manners and she ruled with an iron rod. She was very scary and the gown only added to the image as she wafted over her territory making sure her "girls" were doing their best.
I was hoping to be able to do German since I already had a start but no, it didn't fit in with the timetable so I had to do French with Miss Smith. I was okay at French and worked hard but Miss Smith didn't like me. I had long painted nails and in front of the whole class she made me take my nail varnish off and ordered me to cut my nails. On one of the school photographs I was barred as I was wearing a black bra underneath my custard yellow blouse. She was our form teacher and had done the pre-photo inspection. If I could do it again I would wear no bra as it was cold outside. I wonder what she would have said about that! Despite her, my French oral was not bad and I did love the language lab. Everybody had their own booth and you copied the speech and then rewound it and listened to it. We had had

one at Elgin Academy and the teacher could listen in to any child they wanted to. Did I say a few things I shouldn't have? You can guess the answer.

The history teachers were Mr. France and Mr. Smith. Mr. France was elderly and not charismatic in his teaching. I was becoming unruly and I had chosen my friends unwisely. There was Joyce and Barbara; Joyce was the ringleader, and Barbara and I followed until I found some guts and went off on my own. Mr. France was fair game. I had started smoking so Joyce and I sat in a big bookcase at the front of the class and smoked while the lesson was going on. Smoke billowed out of the cupboards but Mr. France said nothing. Another time we got a bobbin of cotton and would it round the chair legs so he was stopped in his tracks when he paced up and down the rows of desks. He was very knowledgeable but I couldn't respect him as he couldn't control me.

I had a real crush on Mr Smith and always sat at the front of the class even though he spat when he spoke. The syllabus was American History and I found the subject riveting.

Why do they put the worst teacher with the least able pupils? I mentioned before about my poor maths. It was not going to improve with Mrs. Greenhalgh. Joyce and I sat at the back of the room and we lit a cigarette under the lid of the desk. It was clipped in a Kirby grip and we took a drag exhaled into the desk, put the lid down and passed it backwards and forwards to each other. Again she never said a word so of course we lost respect and our maths got worse. This makes me sound like a hopeless case but that isn't true. With Joyce I demanded money with menaces so we could sneak out at lunchtime and buy our 5 Park Drive tipped. Yes, they sold cigs in 5s. Nearly 5p they cost – elevenpence halfpenny and we had to dodge the prefects and make sure we were not seen.

At playtime prefects patrolled the toilets. They made sure that there was only one pair of feet under each toilet. It was very easy to stand on the back of the toilet, so, we smoked in there and passed it to each other. This was a regular occurrence and so it was inevitable we got caught. I think there were 4 of us who were taken to the deputy Mrs. Huddart. I have never fought harder to keep a straight face and I must have been purple. The speech was as follows, "You dirty, dirty girls. Do you drink out of the same cup? Do you use the same toothbrush? Then why are you smoking the same cigarette?" We got the distinct impression it would have been okay to be caught smoking our own cigarette. We roared with laughter and I'm afraid the telling off was completely ineffective. I think this might sound like St. Trinian's but it certainly was not.

Joyce, Barbara and I went to Lewis's which was a large department store. We were in the make-up department eyeing up the Maybelline mascara. We had no money but we took it anyway. Nothing happened and we didn't get caught. My eyelashes were fabulous and we thought we had got away with it. The next day the three of us were summoned to Miss Manners office for an individual interrogation. It appears the security guard saw us and there must have been some arrangement to protect the name of the school and that's why we weren't nobbled on the day. She sent for Mum. I don't remember all the details but I denied it all and called her a liar. She expelled me! Nowadays this would be called an exclusion but Miss Manners was all powerful and could do what she wanted. I got a three-day sentence. This gave me a measure of notoriety and I felt almost untouchable. Well I was now in a different league. I still use the same mascara but now I pay for it and I can honestly say on the QT that I never did it again

There was an emphasis on physical education and competitive sport. In physical education, wearing our grey knickers and yellow aertex tops, we climbed ropes, giggled hysterically on the trampoline, stumbled over the vault horse and performed a variety of rolls on the mat. I once got my knickers tangled in one of the bolts on the top of the climbing frame. I was stuck fast and got a fit of the giggles. The teacher was shouting at me and eventually I managed to free myself but had a hole in my knickers.

We had to go on the bus to Hough End Playing fields for hockey. I was the right inner and wearing my tabard and gym skirt, I had to "bully off" with the opposite member of the opposing team. I loved it and it was a really good outlet for excess energy. Unfortunately, I found it really difficult to control myself and instead of the appropriate bully off- which goes ground, stick, ground, stick, ground, stick, away- I had the tendency to use my stick to do ground shin far too often so I was banned and had my position changed to right wing. Hockey was seasonal so we also played games like rounders and I loved hurdles even if my technique was not good. We had to get the bus to the playing fields as Central was an inner city school and there was no suitable green space. It was on the main bus route so the school didn't have to put on special buses and it was the same for swimming. We got the bus to High Street Baths and went in pairs through the turnstiles into the changing stalls which looked more like Punch and Judy puppet theatres with their striped top curtains and wooden half doors. I like swimming, but here it was very off-putting as there were cockroaches crawling in the changing rooms and floating on the water, so I swam with my mouth closed. The attendants were constantly scooping them off the surface of the water.

On one of our adult reunions, we visited the baths which are now a tourist attraction and won £1 million lottery funding which was only enough to make the roof secure. Most of what went on here was completely unknown to us. There is a four-bedroomed apartment upstairs at the baths and this is where the Baths Superintendent lived. He was a very important man and boss of all the Manchester baths. He had a chauffeur and a luxury lifestyle. Under the baths was the laundry and washhouse. Upstairs there were baths as most of the people round about lived in two up, two down houses with no baths. There were Turkish baths and some of the most splendid stained glass I have ever seen, particularly the angel window. There are fabulous wall tiles and mosaic floors. It is also used for filming and events with lots of weddings but no swimming yet although there are plans for this. When it opened it was billed as Manchester's water palace." The most splendid municipal bathing institution in the country". There were three baths, males first class, males second class and females. Our swimming galas were held in the first class males where there is seating up above. I remember these with bunting draped all the way across, shouting pupils on to the wining line

My favourite subject was Classical Studies or Greek and Roman literature in translation. Our teacher was the fierce Miss Powell who was absolutely inspirational. It took me years of travelling to visit most of the places she told us about. The Cineworld mission statement says "Take me to another world." This subject did that for me so I was off in my head to the lands and stories of Ancient

Greece and Rome. One of the first places I learned about was the Parthenon in Athens, which was one of the seats of civilisation and democracy. The age of air travel and travel agents was in its infancy but I collected travel brochures and cut up pictures of the Parthenon and as many other ancient sites as I could to stick in my exercise book. It's not long ago that I finally made it to wonderful Athens and stood at the top of the Parthenon and looked at the busy city underneath, imagining the goings-on so many years before. We chose our hotel room carefully and had an illuminated view of the Parthenon almost on a pedestal high above the city and it was worth waiting for.

We learned about Homer, the Iliad and the Odyssey; about Romulus and Remus the twin brothers brought up by wolves; Daedalus and silly Icarus who flew close to the sun with his wax wings and fell into the sea after ignoring his father's warning; Medusa, a Gorgon who had snakes instead of hair; Helen of Troy and the wooden horse; Cyclops or Polyphemus the one-eyed giant; Perseus; Zeus and Hades or hell and Ephesus the ancient city and the Temple of Artemis, which is one of the ancient wonders of the world. To see this when visiting and find out there are tunnels under here so the prostitutes can visit the holy men was shocking. I imagined exactly what went on and also scratched my head at the rows of outside stone toilets where the men gathered regularly to do their business in more ways than one!

The story which gripped me most was that of Theseus and the Minotaur and the Palace of Knossos. Crete is one of my favourite places in the world. There are so many historical sites to visit. Heraklion Museum contains many artefacts from a Minoan civilisation. The Palace of Knossos is a ruin but you can still see the bare bones of it with running water and central heating and imagine the bull like Minotaur. In the bay of Agios Nicolaus I could almost see King Neptune rising out of the sea with his trident causing a stir in the water and spilling the champagne in Sly Stallone's glass as he lounged on his huge black yacht which was moored there. This seemed an odd juxtaposition.

The volcanic island of Santorini, which was then known as Thera, impressed me. It's not hard there to find a high vantage point on the island and I could see in the distance all the islands that make up the Cyclades. Miss Powell was the charismatic teacher who did take me

to another place and I'm still going there.
She also taught us English history. I loved the images of Henry V111 and Elizabeth 1 with the ruff round her neck. She funded Sir Francis Drake's trip to circumnavigate the world and bring back treasure from piracy. I learned about Sir Walter Raleigh who brought back potatoes and tobacco; about Christopher Columbus and the ships the Nina the Pinta and the Santa Maria, who were supposed to have found America but actually found the Bahamas. Again I cut pictures out of my Knowledge magazine to illustrate my exercise book. Again Miss Powell enthralled me with her "chalk and talk", her high standards and special brand of discipline.

I could have learned that dead language Latin which doctors once used to write prescriptions so you didn't know what you were getting but I wasn't going to be a doctor so there didn't seem much point. Had I been able to buy an epee and mask I could have learned fencing!

Our school motto was "Et virtutem et muses" which translated means "By by virtue of the muses". That I understood, as they were Greek Goddesses of inspiration in literature, science and the arts. Although there are other versions of the meaning of muses, they all allude to the same ideals.

I preferred sewing with Miss DeVrie to Latin. The practical skills I learned there have served me all my life and I have often made my own clothes and soft furnishings. She helped me make a pair of yellow seersucker pyjamas with black lace. This involved all the skills of cutting and making up a pattern, fitting the garment, sewing French seams and making buttonholes, which are all transferable to other processes.

I was good at biology and remember the lessons about the single-celled organism the amoeba, and about reproduction with diagrams of the male and female reproductive organs in a very perfunctory way unrelated to any emotion but I still blushed. I learned about the make-up of plants and photosynthesis. I still remember drawing and labelling the diagrams. In the cupboard was a real skeleton for demonstration such as showing us the radius and the ulna. I was particularly interested in the names of the bones in the inner ear – hammer, anvil and stirrup, as I had constant middle ear infections as a young child.

Chemistry was exciting and dangerous with its lit Bunsen burners in the lab. We used and pinched blobs of mercury and rolled it round the top of our wooden pencil cases. Many of the experiments we did then would not be allowed now by 'elf and safety. The periodic tables turned me off; I didn't like chemistry and wasn't good at it.

Miss Downs was the geography teacher and she taught us not just about lands and seas but oceans and continents, mistral winds and contours on maps, and the vision of the world in my head was taking shape. We learned about precipitation and the water cycle and she taught us the mnemonic to remember the colours of the rainbow – Richard of York gave battle in vain.

Religious education was also enjoyable and I particularly liked plagues and tempests. I managed to do not only an GCE but a CSE in RE. The school was trying to maximise results but I will come back to this. Re would be my saviour! I was particularly interested when The Byrds released a single called "turn, turn, turn." The words were taken from Ecclesiastes 3:1-8

To everything there is a season, and a time to every purpose under heaven:
A time to be born, and a time to die; a time to plant, a time to reap that which is planted;
A time to kill, and a time to heal; a time to break down, and a time to build up;
A time to weep, and a time to laugh; a time to mourn, and a time to dance;
A time to cast away stones, and a time to gather stones together;
A time to embrace, and a time to refrain from embracing;
A time to get. And a time to lose; a time to keep. And a time to cast away;
A time to rend. And a time to sew; a time to keep silent. And a time to speak;
a time of war. And a time of peace
A time to love and a time to hate;

The curriculum was wonderful and I thrived.

Our different background had always led me to believe I wasn't as good as or equal to, other people. Fiona still says she feels like an alien. I have a friend who also comes from a different background and her parents taught her that to be different was good. I can only think this was all part of Mum's experience about not being good enough.

When I started at the school as the new girl other class members were fascinated by my accent and asked me over and over again to say "rollers and rulers." Scottish people roll their R's and English don't. I didn't like this kind of attention and vowed to change my accent which I did, but put me with another Scot even now and I lapse back, especially on the phone. The singer Lulu says the same. There was a House system to pep up competition and I was in Macmillan, which I thought had something to do with Harold the prime minister, but it was Chrystal Macmillan, who was a Scottish Liberal politician, barrister, feminist and pacifist. Eliot was named after George Eliot, which was a pen name for one of the leading writers of the Victorian era. She was author of the Mill on the Floss, Middlemarch and Silas Marner, which was one of our required reading books. Nightingale was named after Florence and Bronte after the sisters.

In 1964 another new girl joined the class. Her name was Mary. She was beautiful with dark skin and jet-black wavy hair and she wore a gold cross around her neck. Mary and her family had escaped from Famagusta, Cyprus, as there was a Turkish uprising which threatened peace on the Greek side. Eventually the United Nations sent in a peace-keeping force patrolling the border and keeping the Greek Cypriots safe. When we went to Nicosia and looked out of Woolworths first floor window we could see the soldiers marching up and down. I read Victoria Hislop's The Sunrise and I remembered Mary.

No matter how much I liked it I was rebellious and just testing to see how much I could get away with. I wagged school often but usually in the afternoon for the many "dentist appointments", forging cards and brazenly walking out of school. Joyce wagged as well and we would meet up and spend the day in cafes eating eggs, beans and toast and listening to records. I would leave the house as normal in my uniform and start the walk through Whitworth Park. I hid behind a huge tree and watched until Mum and Eric went to work and then went back into the house to get changed. Mum never found out.

School dinners were lively and interesting. I had my dinner ticket, which was the same colour as everybody else's but was emblazoned with Free Dinners. Each table was set for eight people and at one end of the table were the servers. If it was a pie or a cake, it had to be divided into eight. With very dainty table manners several of the girls on the table stuck their fingers into the piece they wanted. I liked the mince pie with a pastry topping, the puddings with pink custard, and Manchester tart with its cornflakes, custard and jam. There was dead fly pie and amputated leg, aka jam roly poly. The noise in the canteen was stupendous. The dinner lady took a spoon and banged it on the Durex glasses for quiet before grace. I should have read it more carefully; it was Duralex, which is just an indication of the workings of the mind of a teenage girl. We knew about French Letters or Durex from Mum.

Everybody in this life deserves the "one significant adult" who believes in them. Mine was Mrs. Johnson, a young English teacher. I wanted to be a stewardess on a ship. "That's a glorified skivvy," she told me. "You can do better than that." She gave up her lunchtime to give me extra English lessons. She wore contact lenses and I was fascinated by her eyes. We read Lucky Jim, Far from the Madding Crowd, A Midsummer Night's Dream with the gloriously named Bottom, Pride and prejudice and Julius Caesar. We all went to see the film with Marlon Brando, with everyone joining in with the speech "Friend's, Romans", so we couldn't hear him say it. We also read Macbeth with the three witches and Northanger Abbey, as set books and we began to become erudite.

In assemblies we all stood till Miss manners came in and let us sit on the floor whilst she was on a raised dais. I loved the hymns, especially the Easter ones, We plough the fields and Scatter, There is a Green Hill Far Away and other like Onwards Christian Soldiers. On the last day of every term we had the tear jerkers, No man is an Island and God Be With You Till We Meet Again.

All Manchester schoolchildren had the opportunity to go to the Free Trade hall for Speech days and to listen to the Halle orchestra conducted by the flamboyant Sir John Barbirolli. It's a travesty that the Hall is now a hotel with just a small shell of the original building left. Now there is the modern Bridgewater hall which is built on stilts.

In the cellar was the sick bay with the nurse and the janitor's quarters. I did get dreadful hormonal migraines and spent time in the sick bay and genuinely didn't feign this. The janitor spent a lot of time in his room and only seemed to come out when we left so perhaps he was intimidated by all the females or he was busy reading The Racing Post.

Then there are the memorable pupils like Marilyn McEwan. She was not in my form, but how could I forget a girl who put Immac hair remover on her eyebrows and woke up the next day to find they had completely disappeared? The fashion was for very thin plucked eyebrows unlike the tattooed handlebars today.

I had to get the 42 or 44 bus home from Princess Street, which runs parallel to Whitworth Street. The school had an excellent image to keep up and certain standards had to be observed and were observed by prefects with black tricorne hats with green rims. On my bus was Athene the prefect, who thought she was perfect and took real delight in reporting the most heinous of crimes such as removing your straw boater or jockey cap. I was not alone in getting detentions and having to write lines, but it was just so boring being good all the time. We always went upstairs on the bus and everybody looks at girls' knickers as they are going up the stairs. Luckily, a company which still exists today made the most beautiful soft lace woollen long-legged thermal bloomers. They were the latest fashion accessory so you didn't mind people looking at your Luxlux knickers.

On the last day of school after lessons were finished and you were no longer going to need your uniform, you came to school dressed a little differently. You wore your thick winter skirt underneath your summer dress. Very bravely at lunchtime we ripped up the stripes on our dresses so they looked like hula skirts. By lunchtime, there was nothing the teachers could do as we were leaving. We went into the front garden and mixed with young men who laid in wait. One of these was a group of photographers and one of the girls went on to marry one of them. We posed for photos and felt a real sense of metamorphosis. The last part of the tradition was to throw your straw boater into the canal along with any unwanted exercise books and watch them float away, symbolising the floating away of school days. I should never have counted my chickens and can't finish this part of the chapter just yet.

Miss Manners was appalled when the education committee decided the school should become comprehensive in 1967 and left to become the head of Felixstowe College for Girls which was a private school. Her claim to fame was the fact that she refused Lady Diana entrance to the school as she considered her not to be intellectual enough. While she was being interviewed Diana refused to speak and kept lowering her head and Miss Manners made her decision based on this.

Chapter 15 Eccentric Eric

Eric had an unusual character and he was the closest thing to a father Fiona and I ever had. I was 14 when I first met him and Fiona was 10. He loved us both but was much closer to Fiona, who he called Bunny. He was tall, balding and had a huge nose. Unkindly, I called him Bald Eagle. He had bad breath and didn't brush his teeth with toothpaste, preferring to use salt. He wore tank tops and a shirt and tie, a casual jacket and trousers. I never saw him wear a suit or anything more casual. I realise I am not painting a favourable picture of Eric, but the saying about never judging a book by its cover has never been more apt. He was a very kind and thoughtful man even though I was an ungrateful teenager.

Mum started going out at night to a club in the city centre called The Ritz. They had a popular weekly singles night which resulted in a few dates. Eric had waited patiently to make his move and they went out one night and came back late. The next day Mum said, "My God, he's got the knack!" It was a funny thing to say and I was shocked. Over time we became closer and closer and were soon what they now call "a blended family".

Eric's taste in food was as weird as Mum's. He lived mostly at the back of the house in the kitchen/diner and we were always made welcome. One of the first of many different flavours was celery salt which is an acquired taste but I liked it. On the cooker was another, very dangerous pressure cooker. It had a very heavy weight to keep the pressure in. Mum and Eric used it often to make almost everything. Mum was making soup when a fountain of liquid spewed out of the top and dripped from every part of the ceiling. It took a long time to clean and I have never risked trying one. Whole meals were cooked in one sectioned pot but it seemed to destroy any taste so maybe that's why he used the celery salt.

The middle room between the kitchen/diner and the front room where all the bric-a-brac was, became The Christmas Room. A house big enough to have a room dedicated to, and only ever used at Christmas. Mum made curtains from a new fabric which was made of fibreglass with a pattern of white with red roses. Eric papered the room and made a fire for days before to warm the room up. Christmas was wonderful. Eric had a hessian sack for Fiona and one for me. They were full of gifts but you had to earn them. He had a pile of home-made cards with instructions on. Things like, sing a song, do a handstand, dance, recite a poem and every time you did it you could take one gift out of the sack. They were all properly wrapped and unbelievably thoughtful and age appropriate. I couldn't believe he had done that for us. A man being kind without wanting anything in return except perhaps a bit of love. I was warming to him.

At the top of the stairs was the room with the chinoiserie wallpaper which I love. It is a style in art reflecting Chinese motifs and decorations like the willow pattern plate but the wallpaper was multi-coloured and stunningly beautiful. This became the ironing room and a lonely looking ironing board was set up near the window. There was a radio for company so Fiona and I could listen to the transistor radio whilst we ironed. I loved radio Caroline broadcasting out at sea. Caroline launched the career of many DJs including Tony Blackburn. As an adult I enjoyed the film "The boat that rocked" which gave a good insight into what is must have been like.

Next door was the bathroom with its medicines. There weren't many but there was Lion's Ointment, Eric's idea of a panacea for all ills. It was an herbal medical ointment used for drawing boils or splinters, or for treating severely dry and cracked skin. The ingredients were lanolin, zinc, beeswax and petroleum. It's still on sale after 100 years.

Up a couple of steps was what had become the bedroom Mum shared with Erico's as she called him. It was huge and had been refurnished and decorated to suit Mum's taste. The furniture was second hand, not because Eric couldn't afford new, but because they believed it was better made. They got two beautiful walnut wardrobes with matching bedside tables and bed.

The big room at the front of the house was seldom used. As I got older and knew more people I asked if I could have a Valentine's party. I was nearly 15 at the time and made a heart shaped cake and iced it but I forgot to put any filling in the middle, so it was very dry. I was never to become a cake maker. There were maybe eight people in the room and it was very innocent; We just listened to music and danced nervously. I also did my sewing here as there was plenty of space to lay out pattern pieces and fabric
.

Our flat at the top of the stairs was where we lived most of the time. Fiona was home from school before me as she could walk and I could get the bus. She was standing in front of the sideboard and I went up to her. She had her hair in plaits and they were alive with lice. When Mum came in and saw them, she was so shocked she took a pair of scissors and cut the plaits off! Poor Fiona. Then she had her hair washed and Mum went to the chemist to get a nit comb and lotion. It took a long time and a red raw scalp before she was nit-free. I was neurotic about Fiona using my comb and brush so I hid them. I didn't want to sleep in the same bedroom in case some of them jumped into my hair.

The bedroom window overlooked Playfair Street. Rusholme borders Moss Side which had a huge Afro-Caribbean population which spilled over into Rusholme. Most of the surrounding houses were terraced and most of our neighbours were Afro-Caribbean or Irish with a few Scottish people as well.

Eric made nettle beer in the cellar. We all helped collect the nettles and get fresh yeast from the baker. The beer fermented in huge vats and the smell was horrid. He also made elderberry wine. Mum was going to check on the beer or maybe she had been drinking some, but she fell down the stone steps and splintered her coccyx. This led to them both becoming more and more interested in herbal remedies and faith healing. There was an herbalist on Great Western Street who sold lots of dried cures, potions and tinctures. Herbalists were once very common and people preferred to go to them rather than the "quack's" modern remedies.

In our living room we had a paraffin heater. One morning when we went into the living room, absolutely everything was black. There were black cobwebs dangling from the ceiling and everything was ruined by carbon deposits which were everywhere. Something had gone wrong with the heater. Paraffin was advertised as Esso Blue but this was Esso black. It took ages to re-decorate and replace the carpets and furniture

Mum was not always easy to live with and she had some of the German traits they are ridiculed for. She was arrogant and often tactless, but most embarrassing for us was the fact that she never learned how to queue. She would just barge straight to the front and get served with only a "tut-tut."
She continued to utter malapropisms and often made us laugh. She listened to the radio and one of the songs was by a group called Los Bravos. She sang, "Black is black, I vont my baby back, und grey is grey since she vent avay." Herman's Hermits had a hit and one line of the lyrics goes, "she's a must to avoid." Mum sang "she's a muscular boy!" She didn't like the Rolling Stones and said Mick Jagger had banano lips. Elvis the pelvis was her favourite especially when he sang Wooden Heart in German.

She liked fragrant men and women. Her favourite perfumes at this time were Tabu and Tweed by Lentheric. Men were wearing Old Spice, High Karate and Brut. Her favourite was Givenchy which she couldn't pronounce, so she said, "Give an inchy," and we added,"and he'll take a miley".
Mum constantly compared the UK with Germany. When we had Beatniks, who Mum saw as deadbeats with long hair, she said it wouldn't happen in Hamburg as they would "hose them down". She was talking about water cannon. The same night there were images of exactly that on TV.

Eric wanted to book a holiday in Riccione, Italy. Mum was a strong character but she still could not make Fiona come with us, so she went to stay with a friend for a week while we flew off into the sunshine. I'm sure Fiona has regretted this all her life as the holiday was wonderful. We went on a boat trip to Venice and enjoyed all the usual tourist sites, but then there were fewer tourists. One of the waiters at the hotel took a fancy to me and he took us all out in his car to San Marino, which is one of the oldest republics in the world. He was called Mario and then he seemed very exotic. I soon realised what they said about Italian drivers was true and we all looked and felt a bit green especially as the car went round bends. It was a lovely holiday and Mum looked happy and very tanned.

Eric bought us a cocker spaniel which was cute but exceptionally naughty. Not only did Lassie eat shoes, but she was partial to walls. As we were all out every day the dog was not a good idea so he was given away. Next we got a cat called Penny. We were out on one of our Sunday trips in Derbyshire when we drove past a farm in Pennistone with a sign outside saying "Kittens." Penny was a tortoiseshell female and the right pet for us. Eric bought pluck for her from Tib Street and cooked it for her.
He bought Mum a moped to give her a bit of freedom but she fell over driving round the garden so it wasn't seen often after that and was stored in the garage.

Eric encouraged Mum in so many ways and even helped her start her own business called "The Crazy Cushion Company." All her designs were registered so nobody could copy them. The cushions were apples, oranges and tomatoes etc. with huge fluttering eyelashes. They were different and Mum even managed to arrange a meeting with one of the buyers in Selfridges in London. It was very exciting as the buyer bought all the samples but sadly no more orders followed. The business flourished for a while.
Eric took us to Llorett de Mar in Spain but this time Fiona came with us. There were lots of cork and olive wood souvenirs. Nobody bothered to use any kind of sunscreen as the dangers of the sun were not then fully understood. Pasty white tourists wanted a tan and some even rubbed themselves all over with olive oil almost as if they were cooking themselves. If you put lemon juice in your hair the sun bleached it without the need to go to the hairdresser.

We went to see a bullfight, or corrida, in the Plaza del Torros. The matador approaches the bull with his red flag and tried to infuriate the bull. When the bull runs after him he has to run faster. Most of the time the bull is killed when distracted by the red flag in a death trust. It is very cruel and Mum knew what was coming as she provided us with a bag to be sick in. Actually we weren't. I won't say we enjoyed it but it was a spectacle I will never forget. The next day we went to a flamenco dance show which was much better.

Eric took Mum to South Africa which was unimaginable to me. She came back talking about the Zulus. It was much better for us that she went on holiday rather than up sticks and leave every time.
Every year on Whit Sunday, which falls on the seventh Sunday after Easter there were enormous processions through the city. Every group and organised was represented. If you were not in the procession you stood to watch it go by in your new white clothes. There were brass bands, church parades, labour organisations, scouts, cubs, brownies and thousands of spectators. It was the biggest event of the year.
The students at Manchester University held "rag week" to fundraise for charities. It was another very colourful events with students pestering everybody for donations and it was great fun. You never knew what was going to come past on the floats or what tricks the students were going to play. Like the walks, it brought the people of Manchester together.

Their favourite place was always Blackpool and in particular in the arcades. They spent hours in there and were worse than children. Eric had saved bags of coins and every penny was spent in great delight. They liked the machine where all the money was at the front and you slid your coin down the chute hoping to push more off than you had put in. There was also one with horses and you backed a particular one to win. The one armed bandit is known as that for a reason but it didn't stop them. Fiona and I got fed up waiting for them to run out of money. We preferred the donkey rides and the "kiss me quick" hats or getting fish and chips. My favourite place now though is the spectacular Tower Ballroom where Mum and Eric danced. I still can't go there without getting emotional. I look at the people on the floor and imagine their stories.

Eric took us to the Blue John cavern in Derbyshire and bought me a necklace with a piece of Blue John in it. We went into the underground caves in a boat on the lake and looked at the rock formations and the stalagmites and stalactites. He told us to remember which was which as tights hang down.
 I got a huge abscess under my arm and had to put some kind of herb in my bra to draw it out and it worked. Eric got more and more

involved with herbalism and self-healing and eventually the garden was deliberately cultivated with nettles.

Everything was hunky dory for a long time until Mum began to believe that Eric was cheating on her - not with a woman but with her business. I have no idea whether this was true or not, but when Mum got a bee in her bonnet there was no shaking it out. As before things went downhill and a divide opened up between them which was to destroy their relationship and result in it being decades before we saw Eric again. Even then it was by accident. Mum was making plans to do a flit but this time it would be on her own as Fiona and I had flown the nest.

Many years later when Eric died someone at the funeral asked what had happened to his herbal books and I had no idea. Another person told me there was a hole the size of a dinner table in the roof of 434. Eric had been living like a hermit. Nobody had been living in 436 for many years and the house looked derelict. Eric slept in a chair and near the end he had some kind of hernia. He told me he had made a truss for himself which the nurses said was wonderful. No doubt it was full of herbs of some description. He died following complications after surgery. He was intestate and he told me he wanted his money to go to the Macmillan nurses and I told him if he didn't do something about making a will it wouldn't happen and it didn't. The house came under the auspices of the Duchy of Lancaster who tracked down some nephews who inherited his money but not before the unsafe houses and had been razed to the ground. After a year's wait we got his ashes. so he is in our garden with Mum in a pot with camellias. As he requested. I half expected them to die but they thrive and I smile every spring when the red flowers blossom. I felt it was the least I could do for Eric. They could have had a lovely life together if they had sorted their differences but remember what I said about Mum not being born to be happy.

Chapter 16 The swinging sixties.

Fashion was changing rapidly with designers like Mary Quant making their mark. London was the epicentre of fashion and if you could get to Carnaby Street this was the nucleus and a mecca for fashionistas. I loved the mini skirt and hotpants which was the uniform for teenagers as everybody wanted to look the same.

In the sixties you had to choose sides, not just for football matches but for music and cults. You were either a mod or a rocker. Mods had short hair and Lambretta scooters and rockers rode Harleys and dressed in leather. You preferred either the Beatles or the Rolling Stones but rarely both. Twiggy was a huge influence with her false eyelashes and pale lips and skin. To achieve this look you needed Max Factor Pan Stick plastered all over your face and lips. Max factor advertised as make-up artists to the stars and we all wanted to be stars. Mary Quant hated stockings and said with the suspender belt they looked like a surgical appliance so along came tights which were much more practical anyway especially if you were wearing short skirts. Hairstyles were back-combed into a bouffant style using a tail comb, sprayed with what was supposed to be hairspray and it held your hair like a helmet. It wouldn't wash out and you needed to use a bath cube and a nit comb to scrape off the residue. My German grandmother had used Elnett for years but this was and still is relatively expensive. I was a rocker and Fiona was a mod.

In some kind of perverse response to Mum cutting off her plaits, Fiona got a friend to give her the male equivalent of a number two haircut which was very very short. She came home sulking and refused to go to school for at least a week until it had grown a millimetre. There was no whitening toothpaste but you could get one which was deep crimson. I daresay it had dried beetles in but it did the trick but making your gums red and therefore your teeth seemed whiter.

I met two young men called Dave and Barry. I introduced them to Mum and she trusted them and was quite right to do so. I wonder now if they were gay as they never had girlfriends and o would have been a good cover for them. The attitude towards gay people then was very different and they would try to keep this private. They chaperoned me wherever I wanted to go and it was usually into Manchester to the clubs, even though I was underage. They came with me and made sure I got back home safely. Eric had no phone at home so when there was a problem there was no way of contacting Mum. Dave and Barry walked me home more than once in the smog. Manchester had brilliant clubs and top artists came to perform in what would be seen now as tiny clubs. The one with the worst reputation was The Twisted Wheel. It was known as a place where you could easily get drugs and in particular purple hearts also known as speed, dexys, black bombers properly known as amphetamines. They were dished out by doctors as a pick-me-up for tired housewives. They were supposed to keep you awake so that you would still be standing all through the night as some of the clubs did. In 1966 on Hastings beach there was a drug fuelled fight on the beach between mods and rockers centuries after the original battle. The pill was supposed to give you "free love" without the risk of pregnancy. In reality most girls were very cautious and I only knew one or two girls who were promiscuous. The hippies talked a lot about free love and they wore flowers in their hair and promoted peace but whenever I saw any they looked stoned. This was the time when Lady Chatterley's Lover was banned for what was then considered obscene but was very tame by today's standards. The game keeper and the Lady stuck flowers in each other's pubic hair and had sex on the forest floor.

My favourite club was Oasis where I saw the Walker Brothers perform "Sun Ain't Gonna Shine anymore; Make it easy on yourself and My Ship is Comin in." It was very exciting. There were long queues outside before the club opened and when you went inside it was very dark and there was no alcohol. Many famous groups including the Beatles and the Stones played there but I missed that boat again. Wayne Fontana played there and he was a local boy.

On 24th June 1964 Joyce and I wagged school but this time Mum sanctioned it. We were going to the TV studio on Dickenson Road to watch Top of the Pops! We spent hours getting ready and queued up with our tickets. The DJ was Jimmy Saville who was regularly seen around the city. The live artist was John Lee Hooker who I had never heard of. He was a blues singer from Mississippi. Much better than that was PJ Proby. He was gorgeous with his long black hair tied back in a velvet bow, he was famous for his tight trousers which

conveniently split on stage. Now he is old, fat and broke but he still has long white hair tied back in a bow.
The top ten that week was
1. You're my world by Cilla Black
2. It's Over by Roy Orbison
3. Someone, someone by Brian Poole and the Tremeloes
4. Here I go again by The Hollies
5. My guy by Mary Wells
6. No particular place to go by Chuck Berry
7. Shout by Lulu and the Luvvers
8. Rise and fall of Flingel Blunt by The Shadows
9. Constantly by Cliff Richard
10. Hello Dolly by Louis Armstrong

John Lee Hooker was at number 31 with Dimples. PJ Proby's Hold Me was not even in the top 50. Wags changed the lyrics to Hold It so that's what we sang.
DLT (Dave Lee Travis) was on Piccadilly radio as a regular presenter and was often seen walking around the city. He called himself the hairy cornflake. I literally bumped into Tom Jones as I ran round a corner as it was common to see famous or rising stars.

I needed to shop and keep up to date with fashion so I had to go into town and work part time. From 434 I walked through the park to get the 42 or 44 bus to Piccadilly bus station. As you got off the bus there were the glorious sunken Victorian rose gardens with bench seating all the way round. It was a very popular place in sunny weather but also at lunchtime where workers could get some fresh air whilst the statue of Queen Victoria turned her back to them. In front of Victoria was a huge Woolworth store on several floors. Years later there was a terrible fire there caused by some flammable furniture material before there were standards. To see a fire salvage sale was common as were the fires. Next to Woollies was Oldham Street. Here there was Affleck and Brown, Marshall and Snelgrove and C and A. the later was known very rudely as c… and as Mum would have said "arsh". The other two were top stores with posh assistants and pushy sales ladies. Affleck and Brown is now the wonderfully eclectic Affleck's palace where you can have a tattoo or piercing and by all kinds of vintage goods.

On Stevenson Square is Fred Aldous which I regularly frequented. You could buy almost anything for making things as it was a proper haberdashery shop. Just a little further up Oldham Street was one shop which would become very important to me but I'll come back to it. Fiona also worked on Oldham Street in a boutique called 2007 which was decorated like a space ship. Back on Market Street was Lewis's department store. For one of my Saturday jobs I worked here on the 3rd floor in the toy department. I wasn't much more than a child myself so this was great. We sold Chad Valley teddy bears and the more expensive Merrythought toys; Tiny Tears and baby Tiny Tears, dolls which drank and weed; Dolls in national and historical costumes; Big hairy Spoofer dogs and I loved it. A member off staff who had just had a baby came in and she brought a rubber ring with her to sit on. My mind boggled as to what was going on in her undercarriage and thought I would delay having babies for as long as possible.

Jobs were very easy to get so when I tired of the toys I went in my lunch hour across the street to another store called Pauldens. They had a job for me so I just didn't go back to Lewis's. On the following Saturday I started work in Pauldens in their posh café called the Veranda Lounge. There was a mezzanine which overlooked the first floor and I became a silver service waitress complete with black dress frilly white cap and apron. This was exceptionally hard work and of course Saturday was the busiest day. Jimmy Saville and a fellow DJ called Dave Eager were regulars. I loved this job and enjoyed working with people, both those on the kitchen side of the revolving door and the customers. I was even allowed to go on the till which took absolutely loads of money and was stuffed by the end of the day. I always made more in tips than the wage for the day but I was whacked with swollen feet when I got back home. After I had soaked them I was ready for round two and off out for the night.

Walking down market Street which was not pedestrianised then, there was another store called Henrys and then a bit further down was Richard Shops which was my next job. I was a teenager in a fashion shop and life couldn't get much better. Every week new stock came in and had to be unpacked so you got first dibs on what to buy with your staff discount. I spent all may wage in the shop and as very happy.

A working girl needs some lunch so I went across the road to the UCP (United Cow Products) tripe shop. I bought potato cakes which I had never had before and apple pies. I lingered over the window. Tripe is the edible lining from the stomachs of various farm animals. There is blanket or flat tripe, honeycomb, book and reed tripe. You have to be a professional tripe dresser to boil and bleach it in preparation for the shop. Well I don't fancy that as a Saturday job! The most common way to serve it is with onions. It needs to be boiled for an hour and a half and there is even a Tripe Marketing Board. It's one food I have never been able to try. The whole of the tripe shop window was filled with the stuff all white or yellow.

Back in Richards in the staff room, I was just tucking into my pie when a member of staff stood on the table to sort something on the message board. She had no knickers on! I mentioned it to her and, very matter of fact she told me she never did.

Right underneath Market Street was a market selling clothes and leather goods. It was very popular and always one of the first places you would go to shop. Sadly, it has never re-opened.

Cross Street is at the bottom of Market Street and there is a little arcade where the Danish Food Centre was. Often on a Saturday Fiona and I met Mum here and had proper coffee and open prawn sandwiches with mayonnaise and lumpfish caviar. This was a little piece of home for mum. On Deansgate was Kendal Milne, which was supposed to be Manchester's finest store. In the food hall we saw Bruce Forsyth buying caviar, not the lumpfish roe we had on our prawns but proper beluga caviar.

Back in Piccadilly at the bus station was a shop called The Milkmaid. This was opened by the Milk Marketing Board to promote dairy products and I got a job here. I learned about cheese – hard cheese, soft cheese, blue cheese, Wenslydale, Caerphilly, Cheddar, cottage, Red Leicester, Lancashire, Gloucester and Double Gloucester, Stilton and Shropshire blue. I worked in the kitchen and waited on and got fat. I made salads to order and the most popular was cottage cheese and pineapple and other salads with grated cheese. I made pancakes with whipped double cream and jam, knickerbocker glories in tall glasses and I really enjoyed it.

I had several clerical jobs using my typing skills that I went to night school for. There were job agencies and it was just so easy. If someone asked if you could do something you just said "yes." When you started the job and were asked if have you used a particular switchboard before, you just said that you hadn't and someone came to show you. I had several jobs as front of house receptionist and usually in solicitors.

I worked in a cotton warehouse called Haighton and Dewhurst as a filing clerk. I sat next to Dorothy. She was dressed in twin set and pearls and she has changed little over the years. This was a great place to buy cotton with a staff discount and I still have a couple of pillowcases and tea towels more than forty years later. These were for my bottom drawer.

One of the longest part-time jobs was on Mount Street by the side of the Midland Hotel. I worked for a man called Anthony Danson who was a surveyor. He was an odd little man who wore a dicky bow. His assistant was Margaret Dagger who collected his rents in cash. I went out with Margaret a few times helping her collect the rents. She took me to her house as she needed to feed her cats and she gave them coley fish.
In the Midland hotel there was a Steiner hairdresser and I spent lots of money there. It was one of the top Manchester Salons and I felt really grown up and decadent going there to have my hair cut and styled like Mary Quant
On the corner of Mount Street was a fabulous old-fashioned tobacconist. The aroma of the tobacco was just divine. I bought my cigarettes there. There was a glass cubicle in the corner which I now know is a humidor and it was full of cigars. As an adult we went to Cuba to a cigar factory. It was really interesting. I'm not sure whether cigars are actually rolled on the thighs of virgins but the workers there are read to for most of the day. At the front the reader sits and serialises books which must be a wonderful distraction to the monotony of hand rolling the tobacco. I knew nothing of this when I was fascinated by the humidor.
The Queen was coming to Manchester to unveil a statue on Deansgate. She came past Mount Street waving and I was really close. It's the one and only time I have seen her at close quarters and

I was taken aback by how much make up she had on. She was absolutely plastered with foundation rouge and lipstick.

Before long Mr. Danson announced that he too was off to be a sheep farmer in New Zealand. He had separated from his wife and I suppose he wanted to start a new life so he sold his business to Joseph Beenstock. He was better to work for as he took me with him when he was doing his surveys and I got to hold the end of the tape measure while having a nosey in some seriously big houses in Prestwich which has a huge Jewish population. I then went back to the office and wrote the reports.

My desk was in the front window and the double decker buses went past regularly. I stated to get some dirty phone calls which was disconcerting. They went on for a few weeks and I didn't really know what to do. I was advised to contact the police and they took it very seriously. I had to annotate the calls which was very embarrassing and then I had to arrange a meeting with him outside Central Library which was scary. CID were all around but didn't turn up and I received one last call from him asking me why I had told the police. He must have been a serial offender and he knew the CID. I was glad to see the back of him even though he was faceless. Another time in Whitworth park a man exposed himself to me and I had to report that to the police but he was another slippery customer who was never caught.

Whilst I'm in Whitworth park, I was crossing the road from the bus stop one day and I was actually on the crossing when a car hit me and tossed me into the air and flung me on to the other side of the road. The driver took me home and left his name and address but I just had a few grazes on my knees which was quite amazing really and no ill effects afterwards.

Eric's factory was on Back George Street which is now the vibrant Chinatown. Eventually his factory burned to the ground a s there was a Chinese restaurant underneath and that's where the fire started.

In Piccadilly there was a shop called Brentford Nylons. The move away from cotton to so called easy care fabrics which needed no ironing, meant people were keen to buy nylon. I can think of few things worse than brushed nylon sheets. If you had hard skin on your feet, you could hear the sheets rasping at night or if you had a rag nail if would rip it off. Often you got your nails or skin stuck on them and they were revolting and when everybody found out for themselves the shop closed.

Manchester had a huge and politically incorrect fur industry and I bought my fair share. I bought a goat skin coat and had Coney (rabbit)jackets. I don't understand how people including myself didn't connect fur with animal. Mum had fox fur stoles with heads on. I sold them recently at a vintage fair so there is still a market. I think it should be like ivory and have a date you can buy them from. The furrier I knew went to live in Spain so he must have made a good living.

As well as the jobs I mentioned I sold Avon cosmetics and its rival at the time Studio. I enjoyed meeting people but knocking on doors and selling is also hard work.

My generation, the so called "baby boomers", seem to have really messed up the planet and at the same time reaped the most rewards financially with houses and pensions. Apologies to those women born after April 1950 who have had their pension ages changed and been robbed of retiring at 60.

I remember watching a programme on TV in the 70s called Tomorrow's World. The presenter was talking about the microchip and telling viewers it would revolutionise our world and it has, but is it better? Only in some ways but I feel very strongly that children have been cheated of the kind of innocent (well almost) childhood I had as they spend too long in front of screens. My grandchildren will have driverless cars and I wonder what effect they will have. The baby boomers have seen more changes than any other generation and I do hope that at least some things turn full circle and perhaps they will. Already there is a demand for all things vintage so who knows, the next trend might be for writing letter with fountain pens.

Chapter 17 Richard Barry.

The 9th February 1965 was one of the most important days of my life although I had no idea of it at the time. Mum had given me advice about choosing boys. Firstly, they had to have good teeth and you would have thought I was buying a horse. Secondly they had to have clean fingernails and thirdly they had to be wearing a suit. Mothers are astute and there was method in her madness. Obviously the teeth obsession was understandable and the fingernails an indication that the person was not a manual worker and the same with the suit.

I was going to Browns to meet Judith from school. Browns was a club in Levenshulme and there were others of the same names above Co-op premises and they started off as dancing schools. Tommy Brown and his wife could see the potential for discos and so they refurbished them and put in wannabe DJ's. I hadn't been here before so was looking forward to it.

I got all dolled up and got the 53 bus literally from across the road on Moss Lane East. Up on the top deck I could see where I was going and at the end of the road the bus turned right on to Wilmslow Road. Almost immediately we hit what is now known as The Curry Mile. Then there were very few Asian restaurants, but it was a meeting place in the late 50's and 60's for the huge numbers of men from the Asian sub-continent who had been invited to work in the textile mills.

At Dickenson Road the bus turned left and soon we were at the BBC studios where Top of the Pops was filmed. It was actually a disused church and the first BBC studio outside London. Dickenson Road crosses Anson Road where there was a roller disco. You hired the skates and they had wooden wheels and the rink was also wooden. It was brilliant and I went there often but today I was venturing further afield. Dickenson Road is exactly one-mile-long and I often use it as a mental measure. I had to get off at Stockport Road and get another bus travelling towards Stockport.

The first interesting place was the ten pin bowling alley. Bowling was popular and I did go several times but it was another sport I was not good at. I got my thumb stuck in the bowling ball and travelled down the lane towards the pins and into the gully. Next to that was the Ten Ten coffee bar which was a real mecca for rockers in their leathers with their huge bikes. It was heaving and intimidating. Almost next door was the Co-op and the entrance to Browns which was upstairs. It was dark with the kind of fluorescent light that makes white fabric really stand out. Girls bras were picked out and almost glowing. Men had to make sure they zipped up after they had been to the toilet or a flashing flap of white stuck out of their fly. It was hard to tell what kind of fabric would do it so you needed to think about what you wore.

There was a small raised area around the sides where the tables and chairs were. At the front was the DJ on a raised platform and at the back was the bar and the cloakroom. We usually drank Coke in a glass bottle with a straw at least until Browns got a licence.

Tommy Brown with his dancing background, insisted that several times every night the DJ played music for a progressive Barn Dance and a Ritz Rhythm which was a jive version. The steps were easy and it meant you got a chance to meet lots of different people as you travelled round the circle. When the music stopped you had a chance to talk to the person who was your partner.

Remembering Mum's advice, I spotted him. He was tall with brown long hair and wearing a three-piece suit which was more than Mum had asked for. We danced and talked and arranged to meet again. It wasn't long before he was coming to pick me up and take me to Browns.

On the 14th February, only 5 days later I received a Valentine's card. It was and still is the custom not to sign the card as you were supposed to guess who the suitor was. All over the outside of the envelope were acronyms. These were first sent by WW2 servicemen to their sweethearts: SWALK- sealed with a loving kiss; HOLLAND-hope our love lasts and never dies; ITALY- I trust and love you; FRANCE- friendship remains and never can end; BURMA – be upstairs ready my angel; MALAYA – my ardent lips await your arrival; BOLTOP, better on lips than on paper. Others too filthy to write. The ones on my envelope were thankfully tame.

Slowly we got to know each other. I was 15 and would be 16 the following month and Barry was almost exactly a year older. He always took me home to the door which meant one bus to pick me up, two to take me there, two to take me back home and one to get himself home. As men did then, he always paid for everything. He told me he had a brother in the RAF but his proved to be wishful thinking as he was an only child. I knew his mother had died when he was about 15 but she too had given him some advice. Pick a girl with long nails and I fulfilled this requirement despite Miss Smith attempts to get me to keep my nails short. I imagined his father all lonely in cravat and smoking jacket in an art deco property with French doors going out into the garden. This was another fanciful idea as Barry and his father lived in what they called a cottage flat. These were council properties where one building was divided up into four flats with two upstairs and two downstairs. Inside the front door was a cupboard which was the coal hole! The kitchen had a range and hanging above was one of those pulley clothes airers which you raised and lowered form the ceiling. In the living room a leather strap used to sharpen a cutthroat razor hung from a cupboard door. The room was simply furnished. There was a cracked and repaired huge teapot on the table with the name Talkes on it which was his mother's family name. This was Measham ware which was popular on the canals. The teapots were made of brown earthenware and personalised as this one was. Barry remembers other Measham items being bartered with the milkman in lieu of payment for bills. His mother and father had married late. When Barry was born his mother was forty and his father was sixty. Downstairs there was a bathroom and Barry's bedroom where he showed me his beermats. I will leave you to decide whether this is a euphemism or not.

By the time I met his father he was retired and aged 76 so Barry was expected to go to work and bring some money in and also to support his father in any way he needed. His father was born on 22nd September 1889, the same date as my son and when his father passed away at the same time as my son was born, Barry was philosophical and said "one out and one into the world."
Barry's dad was born in Stoke and he had three brothers and two sisters. On one day in 1904, the whole family went to the old racecourse in Stoke. There is an entry in Hanley High School log book commenting, "the attendance was very poor. The presence of Buffalo Bill and his Wild West show proved a great attraction for the absentees." The extravaganza embraced 100 American Indians and

Carter the cowboy cyclist. There were re-enactments of wild west incidents and it needed 800 people and 500horses to deliver the show. There were trick shooters; rough riders; stagecoaches; wagon trains; broncos, riding and roping, and even a herd of buffalo. No school could match this once in a lifetime show and I bet an events team would have a job to pull this together today. This was the most exciting thing most people saw in their entire lives and well worth wagging school for.

The rest of his father's working life was spent on the railways as a guard on the trains between Manchester and Crewe. Barry had many gifts of rifles and cowboy outfits as his dad must have remembered that very exciting day. His Mum and Dad also took him to see many Westerns at the cinema so the influence of the show lingered on in happy memories.

I have a photo of me on the settee with my grandparents, Fiona and Mum. I have a new dress on and in hoops around the dress is almost exactly the Wild West scene I describe above. The dress was new and stiff as it had been starched. After washing it would be as limp as lettuce. I doubt there are many housewives now who would get out the packet of starch and use it for dresses or hankies or that other very useful item which was also in the photograph – antimacassars. Younger readers will probably not know what these are. On the backs of settees and armchairs, these pieces of cloth protected the fabric of the settee. There was a hair pomade made of Macassar oil which marked the settee so to stop it they had antimacassars which could be regularly washed. Nearly every train and coach seat has these but they are seldom seen in homes today

Barry's full name was Richard Barry. When I asked him why he didn't use his first name he said he didn't want anyone calling and asking his dad, "is your Dick coming out," and other lewd comments as Dick was the shortened form of Richard. The truth is, many people used their middle name and perhaps kept the first name for Sunday best.

We spent many happy hours at Browns and loved the eclectic music they played, everything from 50's rock and roll to the Mersey beat, MO town plus some rhythm and blues and pop. The DJ we both remember is Raz whose real name was a disappointingly ordinary Ray Birch. He was extremely lanky with long white straight hair and an excellent DJ. Our favourite records at the time were Sony and Cher "I got you babe", and "Baby love," by the Supremes.

On the way home we cuddled at the bus stop to keep warm inside Barry's coat and I started to live in a hedonistic world in my head and my school work began to suffer.

After several weeks of courting I went to see him at the shop where he worked on Oldham street. He had a suit on because he worked in a tailor's shop! It was the rival to Burtons at the time and called John Collier. It advertised on TV and the radio. "John Collier, John Collier, the window to watch," and then a drum roll boom boom a boom, boom boom a boom. The staff in the shop all had tape measures round their necks. Many of the suits were made to measure and gentlemen were asked for their ubiquitous inside leg measurement, and which side they dressed on. When the suit was finished there was a little tab with a button to pull the fabric taught across well, let's just say their bulge. I bet they still do that on Saville Row and other high end tailors but now I think most men have thrown caution to the wind.

Bolts of mohair, linen, worsted wool and crimpelene, which was one of the latest fabric, were piled high in every colour.

Barry wore shirts with stiff detachable paper collars. The collar was the part of the shirt to get dirty first so this was a good way of freshening up. Shirts were made of cotton and needed to be washed and ironed regularly and very few people would have had enough shirts to last till the next washday so, it was a way round it. The cotton mills produced beautiful shirts and the top makers at the time were Tootal and van Heusen. The shop did sell shirts with matching ties and cravats. I learned about pattern making with set in and raglan sleeves, vents in jackets; fancy lining in jackets and waistcoats. It made me think about the clothes I made for myself and used some of these principles, especially the raglan sleeves which were popular.

While Barry worked on Oldham Street, I was at Richard shops round the corner on Saturdays and school holidays. I couldn't wait for the new stock to come in deciding what I would wear to go to Browns. I enjoyed watching the window dressers putting the new clothes on the mannequins. On one occasion there was a model of a red setter and an Afghan hound in the window as they were popular dogs at the time and the window was suggesting you would look great in these clothes with your dog.

As often as we could we went to Belle Vue. It was such a wonderful place and it had never been replicated anywhere although it has been likened to Disneyland. It's a huge loss to Manchester, its people, and all those tourists who came in on the special built railway lines. It was a large zoo, gardens, amusement park, exhibition complex, speedway and stadium and opened in 1836. The things we remember most are the famous wooden roller coaster called The Bobs which hurtled round the very noisy track and the scenic railway with its water splash. It had a flea circus and I never could figure out how you attached a chariot to a flea. It used human fleas which were easy to get at the time. There were elephants you could ride on and take you round the park. It had dodgems with swarthy attendants and a terrifying ghost train. The Kings Hall hosted famous concert artists including the Halle orchestra, Jimmy Hendrix and the Rolling Stones. It was the largest exhibition space outside London. Mum and Eric came here many times to watch wrestling which was a great passion of theirs. Mum got really excited and often stood up shouting and gesticulating about what she saw as fight injustices between the contestants and her favourites were Giant Haystacks and Big Daddy. She did not believe it was fixed. We loved the speedway with its bikes and the dusty stock-cars ramming into each other. There was and still is a dog racing track. It had a boating lake and miniature railway. On a Saturday evening we often went to the Elizabethan ballroom to dance to top DJs like Jimmy Saville and top bands like the Small Faces who sang Itchycoo Park and made it into the top ten in 1967.

Belle Vue had its own brewery and ice cream factory allowing it to have many public houses. The zoo was wonderful and had the highest standard of care and really dedicated keepers. It trained teachers, myself included on how to get the best out of visits to the Zoo with pupils. Catering was a huge problem with so many visitors and the Forte company became involved and this sadly was the demise of Belle Vue. It is said Forte did not want the zoo and in a protest the Zookeepers wore t-shirts saying "don't trust Forte." They were quite correct. Belle Vue started losing huge amounts of money and was wound up in the 70's. It was a very sad day for Manchester and is now this area is a cinema complex and a housing estate. The vision of John Jennison who established the business was dead and many lights went out that night, physically and metaphorically.

At Christmas 1967 we got engaged. Mum was happy with that as she didn't think it would last which was hardly surprising as I was 17¾. In 1968 we went on holiday to Italy. Barry had never been abroad before and I just couldn't persuade him that Italy was hot so he still wore this three-piece bottle green suit and socks and shoes. He said he wanted to see for himself what people were wearing. We flew to Milan which has an amazing vista as you fly into the flat Po basin with the Alps wrapping round it. It was a long drive from Milan to Cattolica and we stopped in the sunshine for a meal with the rest of the coach passengers. We sat outside on laid long trestle tables. First came the chicken dish which I thought was covered with pine needles which had fallen from the trees but I learned it was rosemary. The vegetables were served a long time after the chicken so I wasn't sure if it was meant this way but it was our first real experience of alfresco dining.
Eventually we arrived at the Hotel Lugano which was family owned. The first thing we were told was not to drink the water and everyone knows that now. We loved brushing our teeth with champagne which was as cheap as the water. On the first day Barry put his tie in his pocket and bought some sandals. The next day the waistcoat came off and the button on his shirt was unfastened. After the 4th day he had shorts and a tee shirt. We were only there for 7 days but he needed to learn this for himself. Unbelievably he managed to get really bad sunburn. We met another couple and shared the tiny Fiat hire car to drive all over the place. The car was so small and the guy so tall his head was out of the sunroof like a giraffe.

Barry and his Dad never had a varied diet and in fact it was the same every day – lamb chops peas and potatoes which his Dad cooked. Here he was forced to eat different things like minestrone soup and pizza which he loved and we both enjoyed the chianti. There were fabulous markets with amazing leather goods and the clothes were good quality and excellent design.
It was difficult to settle when we came back home and in the summer I sat my GCEs and didn't do well even though I had studied in the sunshine in the garden. I was tormented with hay fever,

sneezing and itchy eyes. I had a place at Feilden Park Secretarial college and my results were just not good enough to go.
Sometimes, out of failure comes success, especially if you have a pushy mother. Mum had the summer holidays to find out what to do. I was offered a fulltime job at Jardine's book shop which I did consider but I didn't think I was suited to anything which might compare with a library or worse, the image of a librarian.

In September I was marched back to school. It was decided I would stay at school to re-sit the GCEs I had failed and take some new ones on with a view to go to teacher training college which is what I did. It was one time when it's a good job I was easily led. Fiona couldn't wait to leave school and earn money and yet again Mum could not persuade her.
I had to replace parts of the uniform and buy a second hand tricorne hat the same as Dick Turpin and Athene the perfect prefect wore. Some of my fellow pupils were here as they were doing their A levels. I really enjoyed this last year and sailed through my resits. I also did pottery GCE. The teacher was Miss Pearl Isern and apart from teaching us the theory and the practical side of pottery she took us out. We learned about coil, slab and pinch pots, slip clay, glazes, firing and all the terminology of pot throwing; about the history of pots and pots from different countries but most especially English pottery and there was plenty of it. She took us to the Potteries in Stoke on Trent and we had a tour of the Wedgewood factory and watched it being made and the relief applied. I passed with flying colours and had 10 GCEs.

Barry and I began to think about getting married. When Mum found out she went mad and said, "och for Christ sake, don't bleddy marry him go and live with him," which was heresy at the time as there was a real stigma attached to people living "over the brush."

I had been collecting for my bottom drawer for a long time. For our engagement mum bought us a cellular blanket which was the latest thing to have and made with synthetic material. There is a saying, "it sticks like shite to a blanket." It would to those woolly things but with a synthetic one at least it could go in the wash.
Bit by bit and as you could afford it, you bought what you were

going to need. You made your wedding list based on those needs. Gifts were exceedingly modest by today's standards. You didn't have a gift list but if you were lucky you might get a toaster, kettle, clock, iron and ironing board, perhaps some cutlery, towels, plates and very small domestic items. It was long before people expected washing machines etc. but people did not live together as they do now so you were starting from scratch.

I was at Barry's flat one night very close to the wedding. The neighbours must have been watching for us coming out and they gave us a gift of towels and half a pound of rice. The rice they threw over us and it is supposed to be good luck and mean you are never short of food during your marriage. Another neighbour gave me something to hang on my wrist. This had a chimney sweep on which was also supposed to bring good luck.

We had been saving and there was huge social pressure to buy a house. We found a small semi but at the very last minute we decided to blow our savings on a honeymoon and go and live in a rented flat. I bought my dress on Market Street. It was made of shark satin and had 3/4 length sleeves. It cost 5 guineas and a few pearls much to Mums consternation as she was still of the opinion that there would be "a tear for every pearl." I counted them and figured I could cope with that.

We had our so called stag night together with Margaret and John. The roller rink with the wooden floor on Anson Road was now a casino and night club called Oceans 11, serving the snack of the time which was chicken in a basket. We played black jack and roulette and listened to the entertainment and had too much to drink. Barry and John smoked cigars and later that evening Barry was sick and it made his eyes bulge like a frog so it's a good job it wasn't the night before the wedding.

Mum paid for the invitations to be printed and my flowers came from a really posh florist called Dingley's. There were deep red roses and individually wired hyacinth florets. My bouquet was the only thing I had which was really extravagant.

At Easter in my second year at college we got married. Fiona and Margaret were my bridesmaids and John was Barry's best man. On the morning of my wedding, I went for a walk to talk to myself and make sure I was doing the right thing. I walked down Great Western Street to the chemist and bought some Clearasil cleansing lotion. The only answer I could come up with is that I was doing the right thing for now. I couldn't see into the future but I was sure it was right for now. Fiona, Mum and I washed and did our own hair and makeup. Apart from the flowers everything was done on a shoe string. At the last moment Mum had to help me with my dress when I when to the toilet and again she remarked on the pearls on my dress. The something blue was Mums ring from Hartvig.

My 20th birthday is on 28th March. Barry's is on 1st of April and we got married on the 4th so we always have lots of celebrations in one week. If you got married before the 5th April, you got a tax rebate so we just squeezed it in. Mum and Eric were over at this stage and he didn't come to the very small and economical. We married at St Agnes's church in the parish where Barry lived. I was given away by my favourite lecturer Firth Bamforth. Barry's new suit didn't arrive on time so it's a good job he had others to choose from.

After the ceremony we had to sign the register and the pen leaked ink everywhere, luckily not on any of our clothes. Our reception was in a restaurant almost next to Oceans 11. It was such a simple buffet for 32 people. We bought the cake readymade from McVitie and Price. I ate very little and talked to guests. The 4th April was Grand National day and I didn't notice Barry disappear with a friend called Brian. They returned having watched the national at Brian's house a few doors away.

After the reception everyone was invited back to our flat at 434. I got changed into my going away outfit and we went into Manchester to the Wimpy bar and had something to eat. Mum's present to us was a night in a posh hotel called the Queens. It was lovely and luxurious. The following day we got the train to Luton Airport for our honeymoon to Palm Nova, Majorca.

Our honeymoon was fabulous and we even considered running off into the hills and not coming back to the UK. Palma Nova was an underdeveloped resort then and both beautiful and peaceful. Of course I had to go to a Majorica Pearl factory and buy some which I wore for the rest of the holiday. We found Freddie's bar and enjoyed the burgers there which had a fried egg on top. One morning we were there for breakfast when a familiar looking man with a hat,

beard and clarinet came into the restaurant. It was Aker Bilk and his record, Stranger on the Shore was a favourite. He had obviously been performing there and was hungry after working all night.
All to soon we were back on the plane to make our life together in the flat we were renting.

Chapter 18 Mather College of Education

1968-70 age 18-21

Mather was a teacher training college where students could either complete a four-year degree course or a three-year Certificate in Education. It was in the same building where I went to school, just the other end of the building which was once the boys school. There was a shortage of teachers and the entrance qualifications were relaxed and I was one of the few students who did not have "A" levels so I knew I would have to work hard to keep my place and qualify. I am eternally grateful for the grant I received which enabled me to pay Mum rent and buy books and clothes. Upon receipt of my cheque, I had to open a bank account with the National Provincial bank which eventually became Nat West.

All the new students congregated in the entrance hall of the college in September 1968, anticipating the next few years. People chatted nervously to each other and that's how I met Margaret and we were to become a lifelong friends. We were waiting to be introduced to the Principal of the College who was called Miss Murray and she smoked clay pipes. I never thought about it at the time but her partner was her deputy and they were what at that time were referred to as lesbians.

Each student had to choose a main and a subsidiary subject based on the qualifications they already had. That limited my choices greatly. I longed to do art but as I had no art qualifications it was not possible. I chose Divinity, which my Facebook page tells me is an academic discipline. My GCE results made me think this was a good choice as I had not only a General Certificate of Education but a Certificate of Secondary Education so I reckoned I must be good at it.

The subsidiary subject had more options and I fancied the then very trendy Sociology. Margaret had chosen the same and so our paths were set to travel through college together.

"In the beginning," as the bible says, there was me in a twinset and wrap over crimpelene skirt, ready to listen to the word of the Lord in whom I had great faith and two qualifications.

I had always believed the bible was true, as in verbatim so I was in for a huge shock. Our lecturers were Mr. Jones and Dr Harries, a Doctor of Divinity who lived in Skipton which was somewhere I knew with lots of sheep. The curriculum was the Old Testament and in particular the two books Amos and Hosea.

Amos, chapter1verse2; "And the Lord said to Hosea, go take unto thee a wife of whoredoms and children of whoredoms, for the land had committed great whoredom, departing from the Lord." And much more about harlots and nakedness and lewdness.
Chapter 3 verse 11 "whoredom and wine and new wine take away the heart." And more in the same vein. What an introduction to theology and very difficult to understand the meaning which is why we spent months dissecting every word.
The next Book was Amos who was a shepherd.
Amos chapter 1 verse 5 "I will break also the bar of Damascus, and cut off the inhabitant from the plain of Aven, and him that holdeth the sceptre from the house of Eden: and the people of Syria shall go into captivity unto Kir, saith the Lord."
Chapter 9 verse 15 "and I will plant them upon their land, and they shall be no more pulled up out of their land which I have given them, saith the Lord." What would the Lord say now about Syria I wonder? These verses are somehow prophetic and sadly apt today. I'm quite sure we studied many more books but these two were the focus for our exams and ingrained in my memory.
It didn't take long for me to realise that the bible if full of stories written many many years after events. They were reasoned and couched in the language of the time. Tsunamis like the parting of the Red sea were reasoned by the waves being parted by Jesus. We have plagues of insects and frogs now but we can explain them. Very quickly most of my faith in the bible withered so I spent three years studying the wrong subject. I felt naïve and somehow cheated out of my lovely bible stories which I believed to be true. Stories like Daniel in the lion's den, Jonah and the whale, David and Goliath and many more. The New testament could be tracked. I remember seeing evidence of Christianity in one of the temples on the River

Nile on a cruise. Not just crosses carved in to the sandstone but firm evidence of disciples having travelled to Egypt. That really touched me and re-evaluated what I believed in.

It took three years of inner tussle to decide whether or not I was a believer. I do remember discussing as a class Darwin's theory of evolution and the chicken and the egg conundrum.

Whilst we were being indoctrinated at College, not far away on the city streets were men with sandwich boards declaring that "the end of the world is nigh." Others were selling copies of Old Moore's Almanac which gives world predictions based on astrology and it is still published today.

Now Sociology was a different kettle of fish. It fired me up in more ways than one. I fancied one of the lecturers as did many of the female students. His name was Dave Bolton. I enjoyed the many lively debates and began to understand the class system and the makeup of society and families. We read the book called "The family from one end street," which was about a working class family. All other books about families up to this point had been middle class. We discussed social mobility, the breakup of the nuclear family, single parents and broken homes and I could see my place in this structure and I could also see Margaret's. There was an iconic TV programme called Cathy comes home, which was an unsettling story about a couple who had very bad luck, losing their job and home and the children eventually being taken in to the care of social services. It caused a lot of controversy at the time.

In education, we had to learn about child development and prepare for teaching, and in particular the teaching of reading and reading readiness. It was serious stuff but minds drift during lectures especially if you have been into the bar at lunch and had been drinking which was absolutely the norm. The barman on the Students' Union was John who was Irish. We teased him unmercifully and always told him how much we liked his tie but given his Irish nature he was not easily flustered and took it all in his stride. We drank cider or cider with Cherry B, a liqueur which when mixed together were known as knicker droppers. Afternoon lectures regularly passes in a haze and it was a good job there was always a crib sheet for any of the parts we missed.

The lecturers I really liked were Firth Bamforth and Chris Walker.

They were the kind of men who just wanted to do their jobs and had seen all the student shenanigans before.
We went to the Isle of Man for what was called field week even though I didn't see any fields. We took the ferry from Liverpool to Douglas and had three nights in an hotel in Port Erin. We visited the Laxey Wheel, the farie bridge and the parliament known as Tynwald.
Margaret led me astray. She taught me rugby songs like "little boys are cheap today, cheaper than yesterday, standing up or sitting down, little boys are half a crown." She told me they were rugby songs by Max Boyce, but I believe the origin of the song is naval.

One of the students was called Mick. He was a brooding kind of Heathcliff figure who wasn't happy to be there and did his best to separate himself from the group. He sat on a rock with his head in his hand and he just reminded me of Rodin's statue of The Thinker. We saw a policeman and Margaret told me there was only one in the Isle of Man and I believed her. It wasn't the first or the last time she had a laugh at my expense.
There was a dance at an hotel just down the road and nearly everybody went. We met two young men who walked us back to the hotel and we had a snog outside. I could feel his umbrella sticking in me. That really is what I thought and it never crossed my mind it could be anything else. We said goodnight to them and went to our rooms. The next day, there was a letter for me from Barry saying how much he had missed me. In those days first post meant exactly that.
Back at college the work continued and I was not alone feeling really awkward doing dance and being told to be "a tree," and many other things. This was something we were going to have to teach the children so we had to learn to relax into it which eventually we all did.
There were some real characters not only as lecturers but students. I was shocked when Eric continually asked to "screw me" and my mind was launched back to the pig.
Some of the students seem to be a different breed. One in particular was called Pauline and she had a boyfriend with an e-type Jag. He was a pastry chef and worked for his father who had several shops. When she got engaged they went to London to get the ring which

was a large square diamond. For me this was the stuff of movies and really rich people. She belittled me when she found out I used Smash instant potatoes. I thought all students used them. It was food science as they were dehydrated potatoes and I was experimenting!

Naturally she had Cordon Bleu qualifications. I felt mean when I found out that she lived near me and her glamourous marriage only lasted a short while and she told me it was an unhappy experience from the beginning.

There were several students who got married including myself, during the Easter holidays in my second year. After that a big part of our social life was spent in the students' union with John and Margaret who were now engaged.

Now it was important to buckle down and qualify. We were saturated with learning about the 1944 Education Act and the Poor Laws. We learned about the Philosophy of Education and Aristotle's famous quote "give me the child until he is seven and I will show you the man." In other words, the foundations of learning are set at a very early age and as educators we were charged with a huge responsibility.

Every student has to do three teaching practises which are marked and count towards your final qualification. For my first, we had to meet at college at 6.30 am and be bussed out to the deliciously named Oswaldtwistle. This was the first one so much of it was observation, reading stories and supporting in lessons.

The second was a little closer to home at Wilbraham Primary School. The class teacher seemed to think I was there to take over and give him a rest which I was fairly happy to do. Teachers then worked on a topic for a given period of time which they could more or less choose for themselves and I was a lucky girl, as this teaching practise fell exactly as men were landing on the moon. Apollo 11 was launched on 16th July 1969 and the men landed on the moon four days later. Neil Armstrong's famous quote "one small step for man, one giant leap for mankind", was something every child could quote. The astronauts landed back in the Pacific Ocean four days later and it wasn't just the children who learned lots of new vocabulary including, the sea of tranquillity. The children were really fired up watching the news and reading newspaper and it was exciting for everyone and I bet they all remember it now.

My third and final practice was at St Anthony's Primary School and I chose the topic of farms.
We read all about farms and animals and I read them poems. One in particular seemed to strike a chord with one child.
The friendly cow all red and white
I love with all my heart:
She gives me cream with all her might,
To eat with apple tart.

She wanders lowing here and there,
And yet she cannot stray,
All in the pleasant open air,
The pleasant light of day;

And blown by all the winds that pass
And wet with all the showers,
She walks along the meadow grass,
And eats the meadow flowers.

Robert Louis Stevenson
The next day a little boy came to talk to me. "Mrs. Udders," he said. I didn't hear the rest! From fried eggs to udders is a big jump.

Decimalisation took place on February 15th 1971 and was known as Decimal Day. In old money there were 240 pennies were in a pound; 12 pence in a shilling; 20 shillings in a pound; a florin or 2 shillings had 24 pennies. It was a complicated system and to work in a base of 10 is certainly easier but it was difficult for the whole population to get to grips with The new coins were 1,2,5 and 10pence with a 7 sided 50p and still the pound note. It was a huge change but not just for money but also for capacity. The advice was to forget the old system but most people couldn't do that and needed to be able to compare. It was completely foreign and that's exactly how if felt, like being abroad. All computations changed but a base of 10 is easier.
I passed my finals and achieved the status of assistant teacher. Mum was very proud indeed.

Chapter 19. Moorland Road, Didsbury.

1970-1972

Mr and Mrs Smith were there to meet us when we arrived at our new home. It had been a tiring journey back on the train from Luton. After a good sleep we took stock of our new flat which was in the attic of another Victorian villa. We had a bathroom, bedroom and a living/dining/kitchenette. There was one window and a balcony which was the fire escape. The flat was furnished and we were told that our main living room used to house a boxing ring when the previous owners had it.

In a corner was the electric meter which needed shillings in the slot to keep it going. Barry was earning £17 pounds and six shillings per week depending on his commission. I was still a student. We had to start all over again saving for a house but it was as carefree as you could possibly get. Pay the rent, fill the meter and buy food. It was good to have this couple of years without any money worries.

Mr and Mrs Smith lived on the ground floor and they were great. Mr. Smith spent hours in his workshop in the cellar and Mrs Smith always had a fag hanging out of her mouth and as she spoke, the ash fell on to the table. She scooped it up in her hand and dusted it on to the floor.

Mrs Smith taught me about and how to look after houseplants. Who would have thought there was an aluminium plant with silvery aluminium markings on its green leaves, or a prayer plant which closes its leaves as if praying every night? She taught me how to take cuttings in order to propagate plants and this has served me very well. She was green fingered with a bit of yellow from the nicotine.

Underneath our flat were three bedsits which were occupied by the same people all the time we were there. There was one man and a female model who seemed very glamourous and one other student. It was a very happy transient place for us all.

Didsbury is an affluent suburb in South Manchester with a large student population and many bars and restaurants which were very popular and where we spent most of our time socialising.

 It is also the birthplace of the Royal Society for the Protection of

Birds. In 1889 a group of ladies set this up as too many birds were being killed for their feathers.

Going shopping as a married woman was a bit strange to begin with. At the greengrocer I bought green peppers and avocadoes which were new. Most of the food was seasonal so it was good to begin to see exotic fruit and vegetables arrive. Fish fingers and beef burgers were introduced so you needed a freezer but most people made do with the ice box. There were also dehydrated meals available like the Vesta range and Smash! Pre-packaged ready meals were advertised as TV dinners and for some people this meant they would eat meals on their lap whilst watching the box.
A huge second hand bookshop called Morton's served the students well and better still they would buy your books back when you had finished with them. It still exists today.

We bought our first car which an old green mini with the registration plate FLG477B. It was new in 1964. The letter after the numbers only started in 1963, so the letter then, was A. Ours was 6 years old and you could tell. We went to visit Barry's Aunties in Market Drayton. There were holes in the sub frame and Barry felt like Fred Flintstone with his feet so close to the ground he could almost pedal. There was no fitted heated rear window so you had to buy a stick on one which was a poor substitute.
We went to visit Fiona and her husband Ernie in their high rise flat in Blackely. Mum was also there in another tower block. The planners of the time thought it wise to get rid of terraced houses and build tower blocks which had all mod cons. They did however throw the baby out with the bathwater doing this. Many people became isolated in them and the lifts often broke. Not everyone could climb up or down the many flights of stairs and there were far too few open spaces. Fiona seemed okay here with Ernie but Mum was sinking. She worked at Kendal Milne. She suddenly decided she was moving back to Germany which was a real shock for us. Our Mummy was abandoning us but we understood why and just wanted her to be happy.
She got a flat and went to work as a translator for Hapag Lloyd and she loved it all, the flat, her job, the lifestyle and she seemed to recapture some of her lost youth. She went on many dates including

one with a member of the Schwarzkopf dynasty, but he bit his nails so that was the end of that.

I went to work at St Philip's primary school in an area in the centre of Manchester called Hulme. It was easy for me to get the bus there and I enjoyed my work very much. This was pre-national curriculum so there was freedom to teach what you wanted as long as you got the results. You were expected to teach children to be literate and numerate. Expectations were passed on from one teacher to another and there was an unwritten curriculum. St Philip's was a multicultural school with a great deal of pride and poverty in equal amounts.

The population was growing and there were many prefabricated classrooms in playgrounds and they were heated by electricity.

In 1972 the National Union of Mineworkers were in a dispute with the Conservative government of Edward Heath. It was the first time since 1926 that the miners had been on strike. The National grid had to ration the electricity and we had power cuts for hours at a time. There was no way to spare schools so when the power went off it was a case of coats on and huddle together. The electric heater in my classroom didn't work and everyone was freezing. These children were 6-7 and you just had to get on with it.

I was really upset when I lost my engagement ring. It must have come off in my glove and was never seen again. I had to claim on the insurance and the one I got was bigger and better but certainly not the same. In houses everyone had candles at the ready and the TV going off made the birth rate spike. Eventually the strike ended.

Barry's attempts to teach me to drive, ended up with me abandoning the car in the middle of the road and leaving him to it. Lessons came after that and I passed at the second attempt. My friend Margaret's father had given her his old Morris Minor for her 21st and I was very impressed. I had a party for 21st birthday in the flat. I got the latest record player on a tripod stand, a watch from Mum but no car.

After renting for two years, we saved a deposit and we bought our first house.

Chapter 20. Brandon Avenue, Heald Green.

Heald Green was in Cheshire when we moved here as part of Cheadle and Gatley Urban District Council but under boundary moves it became part of Greater Manchester under Stockport Council.
Manchester Airport is owned by the Manchester City Council and is one of the largest employers in the area. Although it was the tiny Ringway Airport when we moved in, it has grown into Manchester International Airport with three terminals and plans to grow even bigger. Heald Green and the surrounding areas have a transient population mostly due to work at the airport. In agent speak it is a very good location, not just for the airport but the excellent links to the M60, M62, M56 and M6. The infrastructure has developed enormously in the time we lived here.
If you do live here, you have to like planes as we are on the flightpath and planes fly directly overhead.

In the words of the Manfred Mann song we had become semi-detached and suburban in our 1960's Wimpy house which we bought from Mrs. Brindley who was a domestic science teacher at Central for Girls. We probably only owned the front door and would spend the next donkey's years paying off the mortgage. My salary was exactly the same as the mortgage - £68.68, which is not a number you are likely to forget. We bought G-plan dining room table and chairs, a "matchbox" washing machine and a settee from the Ideal Homes Exhibition. The Brindley's left full length lined curtains and a grass green velvet Wilton fitted carpet which had similar attributes to grass. It had the kind of pile which showed every footprint and when you hoovered, it striped like grass and drove me mad. I had to hoover in the same direction to avoid the stripes and although it was an obviously expensive carpet I couldn't wait to get rid of it.

I got a job a bit closer to home in Handforth as it was really difficult to get to Hulme as I hadn't passed my test yet and didn't have a car. I was introduced to the headmaster who was looking for a member of staff and he offered me the job. There was no interview, or application form, just a recommendation. I needed to show my Teachers Certificate and National Insurance number. He lived just round the corner and his name was Mr. Doleman. I worked at the Grange County Primary School which was very different from the one I had just left and with middle class parents having high, sometimes too high expectations of their children.

One of the teachers was Robert Millard. He was a moody man but his saving grace was the fact that he was an excellent pianist. Grumpy in the morning he would go into the hall and blast out Nutrocker by B. Bumble and the Stingers. He played standing up like Jerry Lee Lewis and I loved it and often asked him to play. Before the children came in he walked around school smoking his pipe.

Women were just beginning to wear trousers and Mr. Doleman told me if I wanted to wear trousers then I would have to wear something to cover my bottom and I wondered what weird pervy thoughts were going through his head. He was also moody and you could tell which way the wind was blowing by the way he had combed his hair. I felt I was working really hard and asked him for a pay rise. He told me that nobody was indispensable and that was the end of that.

Fiona's husband Ernie was a painter and decorator and he did a lot of work for us. Fiona brought Louise her young daughter and they stayed the night on several occasions. Louise found a bottle of perfume called Devon violets and managed to spill all of it in the bedroom. The sickly smell was in the house for days

We went to the local hardware shop. We bought ladders and I asked for a stretcher. "we don't have any of those love. You will have to go to the hospital for that," the man said. After describing what I wanted he said "ah, you mean a prop." Mum again! They had always been stretchers as that's what they did to the washing line.

Nearly every time I hung out the washing I had to wear wellingtons as the clay soil was either cracked and baked in dry spells or swimming with water. I watched the planes fly over and imagined the destinations they had come from or were going to depending on literally which way the wind was blowing as planes have to take off into the wind.

The planes have also changed a great deal. They used to fly all through the night and no regard was paid to the quality of sleep people had. The airport is a responsible employer and provided huge grants to people living on the flight path so they could have secondary glazing installed to cut down the noise. Plane manufacturers made quieter planes and now they rarely fly during the night.

Planes are still noisy when the weather is wet. The strangest noise they make is the vortex which is a real shock when you first hear it. It is the equivalent of the wake a ship makes but obviously it is in the air and you can't see it. It whooshes for ages, shakes trees and bushes and can cause real damage to property. Our next house was affected by this. I came home one day to find many of the tiles standing on end and a huge hole in the roof, although not quite the size of a dinner table. The moss was gathered in the vortex and swirled around the chimney mostly landing on the neighbour's brand new white Range Rover. Behind his car were four broken slates which just missed. The airport sends out surveyors to identify vortex damage and in time you get a new roof. There must be hundreds of people who have had new rooves.

Many airlines have gone bust over this time, Clarkson's and Laker airways to name a couple. The Red Arrows used to come over more often than they do now but one of my favourite planes was the Vulcan Bomber. It recently did a last flypast and we looked out of our loft window and watched it come over our roof and we literally waved to the pilot.

We loved Concorde and the noise it made coming in could be heard for ages before it was seen giving plenty of time to rush outside and watch. The airport has an Aviation Viewing Park and there is a retired Concorde in a huge hangar there and it still looks special. I was on playground duty at a local school and watched a plane come in with the space shuttle piggybacked on top. It was also destined to be an exhibit at the airport. My absolute favourite was the Guppy, named after the tropical fish. There were five of them and they were wide-bodied cargo planes used to transport aircraft wings from Toulouse to Manchester. They were the strangest planes ever. You see, you really have to love the planes if you live here.

Back down to earth we took Louise who was a tiny baby to an open air pool in East Didsbury. It was a lovely day and thousands of wasps were joining in with the swimming. There was a café and ice-cream on sale but how many days like that do you get? The pool is now the car park of the gym we go to.

Barry and I had a meal out at Toby Inn when he announced out of the blue, that he had always wanted to be in the police. At John Collier there was constant pressure to improve sales figures each week and it was getting him down. So he applied for the police and off he went to Police Training College for six weeks after he passed the entrance exam. He had to complete a lifesaving qualification and have his hair cut in a short back and sides which was not the fashion at the time and a sacrifice for him. I remember the day he stood in the back garden in his uniform with his truncheon and we took a Polaroid instant photo.

Next door another young couple came to live called Pauline and Tony. There was some competition between us and I suppose it was an era of "keeping up with the Jones's." Pam and Mike came to live in the adjoining semi and we socialised together and started bringing up families.

Mum came over from Hamburg regularly, and she always wanted to be taken out which is not the easiest thing to do when you are working full time and exhausted.

Barry got fed up being on his own when it was parents evening so I took him to the local pub whilst I went to school and then met him afterwards. Here he met a neighbour called George who lived next door but one. George was a widower. I picked them up and took them both home with fish and chips to soak up the alcohol. I thought Mum would like him and he agreed to a blind date as Mum was coming soon.

George was tall, well dressed with a trimmed moustache and educated and he worked as a draftsman for the Post Office

On 19th December 1974 we all went to a local hotel for an Xmas night out and a blind date. We got a mini-bus to take Mum, George, Pauline, Tony, Barry and I to The Valley Lodge Hotel. As corny as it sounds, Mum and George danced and you could just see the chemistry between them. By the end of the night we were talking about marriage. None of us had ever seen "love at first sight".

They had a few days before Mum went back to Hamburg and when she returned George followed her and things moved quickly.

It was very difficult for Mum to get a divorce but George helped her and before we knew it, Tony had arranged through his air cargo firm for a huge container to be collected from Hamburg and delivered to 62 Brandon, next door but one to us. Her furniture was amazing; we hadn't been to Germany to her apartment so we had no idea what it looked like. Her suite was huge and she also had what she called her shrank. It was a wall unit the size of a long wall and I have still never seen anything like it. She transformed George's house and soon they were to be married.

In the mean time they settled together and every weekend George washed his pale blue Ford Capri which he loved. He had been a church organist and treated himself to a home Wurlitzer organ. They both sat on the stool and George played while Mum listened or sang or played her mouth organ. Sunday lunches at the pub were followed by this ritual.

George had a tattoo on his forearm of a Grenadier guard. I imagined him in his uniform and busby. He told me he had had it done when he was drunk so it was another illusion shattered.

It was a real surprise when we found out that George's family were German. The Wagner's arrived in the mid-18th century from Hollebach and Munchenburg. Germany was struggling and England was benefitting from the industrial revolution. They were economic migrants and some went into the lace industry around Nottingham while others went to Yorkshire to become master butchers. George's fathers hard work helped him become established in Lancaster as a master butcher. The Wagner's suffered abuse around the time of WW1 and decided to Anglicise their name to Warner. So George was half German, as Mum said, a mongrel like we were.

George and his sons, Shaun and Neil along with Tony, Ernie and Barry all went to the local pub for the stag night. Everything was fine until a man came in and he was taking pictures with his monkey. Barry had the monkey on his hand and it slipped and rolled over and must have been scared, as it bit him. I remember him coming back from the pub drunk with his finger in the air saying "I've been bitten by a monkey!"

The ceremony was at Stockport registry office and the reception at the Bamford Arms on Stockport Road and it was a happy day for everyone. It was April and just four months after they met. Mum was 53 and George was a similar age.

Mum and George drove off to Harwich on the ferry to Hamburg and their favourite spot on the fish market for a few lidded steins of Holsten.

On their return Mum was on her way again but this time because George was promoted to Allerton Yorkshire where they lived in a beautiful apartment overlooking the moors and very close to Bronte country. We went to visit several times and spent a couple of Christmases there and the scenery was beautiful.

In the winter, if we had one snowflake at our house, Mum was completely snowed in and so she had come full circle as George had to shovel them out just like Glenfarclas. I think it was here they were the happiest. George had been commuting every day on the awful M62 motorway so it must have been a relief not to do that journey.

Eventually George's work brought them back to Manchester. They bought a flat in Sale which was the home of the Sale Sharks Rugby Club. George had missed this so now they took full advantage of being within walking distance so they could watch the match and enjoy the celebrations or commiserations afterwards. I remember going a couple of times and being fascinated by some of the player's huge upper bodies and cauliflower ears.

When George retired they moved to a house with a garden where they had a few years happiness. On one very special holiday they went to Sao Paulo, Brazil to visit Neil and his wife Jo. They came back and set up Caipirinha cocktails to drink every night. It's Brazil's national drink and made with lime, caster sugar and cachaça on ice.

Mum managed a subsonic trip to London on Concorde which she loved. I have no idea why George didn't go with her but he was a Yorkshire Man and they are known for being mean.

Her Copd (Chronic obstructive pulmonary disease) deteriorated and affected travel plans. She still went back to Germany but now usually alone. She would only fly Lufthansa, the German airline but it was not a cheap flight as it is now. She needed to carry a heavy oxygen cylinder with her and always had to pay for two seats. Eventually every time they went on holiday Mum ended up in hospital. There were no mobile phones then so I just waited for the call every time wondering what was happening. The time came when her travelling days were over.

George developed epilepsy and spent countless hour typing perfect letters to various epilepsy associations.

Sadly, they both ended up in residential care paying a fortune for fees after living a frugal life. Care home fees in Scotland are still free. When they both passed over, George first and then Mum I had to make sure they both had exactly the same coffins or there might have been bickering which was what held their marriage together for many years. George called Mum "the director" or, "the pendulum" depending on her mood. Mum had been saying for many years that she was growing back into the ground, ashes to ashes style. She always believed in the afterlife and said she would come back and give us some sign if she could. She didn't.

Barry picked me up from school one day and I looked in the rear seat. There was a plastic sweet jar carefully safety belted up. "What's that?" I asked. "Your Mum" he replied. He had been to the undertaker to collect her ashes. She would have really seen the funny side of that. Mum wanted her ashes in our garden. "Put them somewhere the cats won't pee on me," she asked and I did. For Mum it was journey's end. George went back to a favourite spot in Lancaster.

Now when I go to the Tower ballroom in Blackpool, I see Mum and Eric dancing and George rising out of the bowels of the theatre playing the might white Wurlitzer.

Printed in Great Britain
by Amazon